FROM BOMBS

to

BOOKS

FROM BOMBS

to

BOOKS

The remarkable stories of refugee children and their families at an exceptional Canadian school

DAVID STARR

JAMES LORIMER & COMPANY LTD., PUBLISHERS
TORONTO

James Lorimer & Company Ltd., Publishers acknowledges the support of the Ontario Arts Council. We acknowledge the financial support of the Government of Canada through the Canada Book Fund for our publishing activities. We acknowledge the support of the Canada Council for the Arts which last year invested $20.1 million in writing and publishing throughout Canada. We acknowledge the Government of Ontario through the Ontario Media Development Corporation's Ontario Book Initiative..

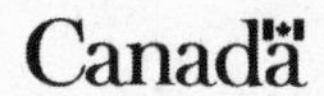

Canada Council for the Arts
Conseil des Arts du Canada

Cover design: Meghan Collins
All photographs in this book appear courtesy of Lisa Snow and Jennifer Houghton.

Library and Archives Canada Cataloguing in Publication

Starr, David
From bombs to books : the remarkable stories of refugee children and their families at an exceptional Canadian school / David Starr.

Also issued in electronic format.
ISBN 978-1-55277-860-9

1. Refugee children--British Columbia--Biography. 2. Refugee children--Education--British Columbia--Burnaby. 3. Refugees--British Columbia--Biography. 4. Edmonds Community School (Burnaby, B.C.)-- Biography. I. Title.

LC3665.C3S73 2011 371.826'9140922711 C2011-904414-5

James Lorimer & Company Ltd., Publishers
317 Adelaide Street West, Suite 1002
Toronto, ON
M5V 1P9
www.lorimer.ca

Printed in Canada

This book is dedicated to

The men, women and children whose stories lie within these pages: your courage, grace, and dignity inspire and humble me. Thank you for sharing your words.

The staff of Edmonds Community School and Byrne Creek Secondary past and present: the finest educators in the province.

My Parents: my first and finest teachers.

My wife Sharon: both my compass and my Northern Star. Thank you for your editing prowess and your patience, understanding and love. This book would not have been written without you.

My children Anthony, Nicholas, Justin, and Aidan: may all of your journeys end in safe harbours.

Once you choose hope, anything's possible.
—Christopher Reeve

CONTENTS

LOVE SURF
malibu beach
since 1982

Byrne Creek Secondary's theatre, the Centre for Dialogue, is full of students, parents, and school district dignitaries. The annual Grade 7 public speaking competition finals are about to get underway, with the best eight orators from among the more than two thousand students from the district's forty elementary schools set to compete for the championship. The host stands up, the audience settles, and one by one the speakers step onto the stage.

This year's theme is *Imagine*, and for the next two hours or so the finalists will orate on that subject, imagining a world without fear, disabilities, poverty, and disease. I listen attentively to the speakers and they are good. Very good.

Their enunciation is crisp and their vocabulary broad and expansive as one by one they orate on their chosen topic, receive their applause gracefully, and then sit and listen politely to the next speaker, all the while judging themselves against their competition, hoping for the coveted trophy.

And then it's Elaha Anwary's turn. Elaha is from Edmonds Community School. She is a compact, thirteen-year-old Afghan refugee with dark eyes, shoulder-length black hair, and a serious disposition that belies her sharp wit and sense of humour. Elaha has been in Canada since she was six, but she is still more comfortable speaking in Dari or Pashtu than English and, although she does her best to cover it, those who know her can tell that she's very nervous.

Elaha, however, is not the kind of student who lets a little thing like nerves get in her way. She is a driven, determined girl with straight A's, and she's been practising her speech for hours each day in front of the mirror or to her family and friends ever since she won the zone competition and the right to attend the final. Winning this competition is something she wants, but for different reasons than most.

She wants to win to make her parents proud, that much is obvious, but she also wants to show them that the great sacrifices her family made to get out of Afghanistan have started to pay off, and the Dave Carter Cup—the silver bowl named in honour of the teacher who started the public speaking competition more than two decades ago—will do nicely for a start.

Elaha also wants to win for her school. It's a big thing for an Edmonds student to make it this far in this competition—in any competition, for that matter—and it's not the sort of thing that people expect from Edmonds. Very few

Edmonds students have reached the public speaking final and certainly none have won it. Traditionally, the winners, it seems, have come from other schools in wealthier, "better" parts of the city.

Elaha makes her way to the stage, waits for her prompt, and begins to speak. Her topic is "Imagine a world without war" and, within a few seconds, the audience realizes that something very special is taking place. Kids often orate on weighty subjects like war at competitions like this, but with Elaha it isn't war in the abstract. Elaha is speaking about war from a personal perspective—a profoundly, deeply personal perspective. Her voice wavers as she tells the hushed crowd of her grandfather's execution by the Taliban and of her family's subsequent exodus from Afghanistan, but she keeps her emotions in check and finishes strong, her powerful voice enhanced by the great acoustics in the room.

For a second or two there is no response. This is not, it would seem, the sort of thing a thirteen year old should have any experience with, and it takes the audience a short while to react. And then the applause comes—long, loud, and sustained. Many cry, myself included. The other students finish their speeches, and then the judges retire to consider what they've heard. Ten minutes later they return.

The audience and the students sit down and listen attentively as the third place and second place are announced. They are good choices—the speeches were excellent and the names are received with enthusiastic clapping—but, as the winner is announced and even before Elaha's entire name is read, the place erupts in cheers. As I stand and applaud, I can't help thinking how fitting it is that she has won this trophy at Byrne Creek—the school she will attend next year, and the one that, even three years after I left, still holds a place in my heart.

Elaha's father and mother weep unashamedly and hug their daughter. Dino Klarich, Edmonds' Vice Principal, and Edmonds' teacher Karolyn Washtock smile proudly as Elaha makes her way to the stage. She receives her trophy and stands graciously with the second- and third-place finishers, congratulating them on their speeches, all the while beaming for the cameras. Ahead of Elaha now are a series of public engagements: speaking at the school board, for the retired teachers, and for the District Parent Advisory Council. Her victory has made her a minor celebrity in the district, and she accepts the duties willingly.

It is a moment of unbridled joy and immense pride for all of us who know her, and as I look at Elaha on the stage I know beyond doubt that this is a child who, in the words of Elin Horton, Edmonds' Head Teacher, "is a kid with quite a future ahead of her."

The crowd thins, parents and students depart and, as I walk out of the Center for Dialogue, an individual approaches me and shakes my hand. "Good for you and good for Edmonds," he says. "Winning is a pretty big deal for one of *your* kids."

One of your kids. It was meant to be a compliment no doubt, but the comment came loaded with the prejudice and preconceptions people across the city have had about Edmonds for years—the ghetto school; the refugee school; the last-place-in-the-rankings school—as if success for these children was something unexpected, conceded grudgingly to a school that didn't deserve it.

"What do you know about my kids? Who are you to

stand in judgement of them? What right do you have to criticize these children?" These were the things I felt like saying. After all, I'd heard comments like this before and hadn't been shy about rising to the defence of Edmonds. But I was tired and I had an important job to do before I could go home, so I just smiled, thanked him for the kind words, and bade him goodnight.

But in the car I seethed. I wasn't surprised Elaha had won. Hell, I'd have been shocked if she hadn't, but the preconceived notion this person, and many others, hold about Edmonds and its students still rankled me. *One of your kids.*

One of my kids? I thought. Let me tell you about my kids. About their families and their lives. About the sacrifices they made to come here. About the courage, resiliency, and determination it took for them to make it against staggering odds. About how hard the teachers at my school work, every day, to support kids who could so easily fall between the cracks. Just let me tell you.

Elaha Anwary with the Dave Carter Cup

1
FROM MANY PLACES

Edmonds Street has always been a place of new beginnings. The Scottish, Irish, and English arrived here more than a century ago, soon followed by successive waves of Japanese, German, Italian, and Polish immigrants. In the 1970s and 1980s the Indians and Chinese came, joined by Bosnians and Croatians, Koreans and Filipinos. Today the neighbourhood is an assortment of small shops and businesses that speak to its current demographics: a Balkan butcher shop next to an Afghan restaurant; an African grocery store adjacent to a tattoo parlour; a temple across the street from an adult video store, the call to prayer competing with pornography.

Edmonds lies in the southern corner of Burnaby, British

Columbia, a wealthy suburb of Vancouver, a city of glass towers and snow-capped mountains, still basking in the after-glow of the Winter Olympics. Although it has long been the poorest part of town, new development is finally happening after years of neglect. Condominiums are taking over the vacant lots once occupied by boarded-up buildings and crack houses. New businesses are tentatively opening along the street. These slow steps toward gentrification notwithstanding, this neighbourhood is still a rough place—a place where newcomers and third-generation residents alike navigate the landmines of addiction, violence, and poverty.

There are many problems in the neighbourhood, but it is still a tight-knit community—one in which residents take pride. That pride is evident in the regular neighbourhood cleanups, in the Santa Claus parade, and in the faces of the children who attend Edmonds Community School. In a profoundly personal and concrete way, that school represents the most distinctive aspect of the community: the dreams of a better life that the refugees and immigrants who live there have carried with them from their homelands.

From the outside, Edmonds Community School isn't much to look at. Originally founded in 1894, the school is housed in a two-storey white-and-green building that was built just after the Second World War to accommodate the growing number of families moving into the neighbourhood. Over the years, the school has counted several famous people among its alumni, including Carrie-Anne Moss of *The Matrix* and Hollywood star Michael J. Fox. But the neighbourhood and the school have changed a great deal in the almost forty years since Fox attended, and the only artifacts left of him are yellowing class rosters and an old yearbook photograph.

Edmonds lacks the flash of newer schools in other parts of the city and, despite recent updates, the place seems a little tired. The pavement in the parking lot is cracked, the playground needs upgrading, the gravel soccer field has a habit of flooding in the winter rains and, last year, a cherry tree on the south side of the school—one of the few green things left on the grounds—fell sick and was chopped down. Edmonds is, from the outside at least, a fairly ordinary place. But looks can be deceiving.

The view from inside the front door is very different. The school is spotless, with new flooring throughout. Artwork covers the walls and, in the foyer, there is a beautiful mosaic that encapsulates the school's demographics. Colourful clay tiles surround a map of the world and earthen "luggage tags," one made by each student in the school, cover the walls. In 2009 Keith and Celia Rice-Jones, well-known Vancouver-area artists, were commissioned through the Artist in Residence program to make the mosaic, entitled *From Many Places*—a fitting choice, since the school currently serves students from almost fifty countries.

During its recent history, the school has become a remarkable experiment in multicultural education, tolerance, and diversity. Nearly 100 students of refugee families from countries such as Ethiopia, the Congo, Sudan, Somalia, Uzbekistan, Afghanistan, Syria, and Iraq now call Edmonds their home. The school and the refugee population it serves have frequently been featured in local, provincial, and national media. The Burnaby *Newsleader* and Burnaby *Now* have run articles about Edmonds, and the Vancouver

Sun recently ran a comprehensive series on refugees in the neighbourhood that spotlighted the critical role the school plays in supporting them. Edmonds has also been prominently featured on Global Television, and twice in three years the Vancouver *Province* ran positive articles about the school's diversity and its students' athletic prowess.

But there has been negative publicity as well. The Fraser Institute—a right-wing think tank that takes assessment numbers from the controversial Foundational Skills Assessment (a reading, writing, and math assessment written by students in Grades 4 and 7)—has singled out Edmonds as one of the "worst" schools in British Columbia. Traditionally, the school ranks low in these assessments—not just low, but very low. The school was fourth from the bottom on a recent "report card," and the rankings have always been a source of anger in the building.

Why do I care so deeply about Edmonds' scores? I care because I am the principal of Edmonds and because the Fraser Institute's assessment is simply wrong. In my view, the rankings misrepresent the truth about my school. Far from being one of the worst schools in the province, Edmonds is actually one of the best at what it does.

The Fraser Institute fails to take into consideration some essential realities: six-out-of-ten Edmonds students are currently still learning to speak English as a second language; eight-out-of-ten don't speak English at home; and fully one-third of our students come from refugee backgrounds and often arrive at the school at ten, eleven, or twelve years of age having never attended a school before.

And these are only a few of the special circumstances that affect our students. In many cases, they have witnessed scenes of horrific violence and bear the scars of significant physical and psychological trauma. Yet when these students reach the school, they are welcomed by the open arms of staff members who, with a skillset second to none, start them on their journey through the school system. Often new students can neither understand a word of English nor read or write in their own first language. Yet, with just one or two years of instruction, these children learn to function proficiently in English and find themselves well on their way toward catching up to—and frequently exceeding—their native-born peers.

In some ways, I came to Edmonds with almost as much to learn as my students. I have lived in British Columbia since the age of four, when my family emigrated from England. I was educated in a small rural high school and then at Simon Fraser University and the University of British Columbia. I spent eight years teaching social studies and English literature in the comfortably middle-class suburb of Coquitlam, and then—armed with a newly acquired master's degree in Administration and Leadership from UBC—two years as an administrator, a year as a vice principal, and another year as a principal in a small rural public school in the eastern Fraser Valley.

My first two years as a school administrator involved a learning curve like no other I've ever experienced: school finances, law, dealing with difficult people, and working with social services, the police, the First Nations bands, and a host of community partners was an education in itself. But when I began working as vice principal at Byrne Creek Secondary School in 2006, it was immediately clear to me that small-town schools with predominantly white and First

Nations students were worlds apart from the large, urban, multicultural community where I now found myself.

To begin with, my background made me the quintessential fish out of water. But then something happened. Simply put, I fell in love with Byrne Creek when I realized just how important the school was to the families and students who attended it. I got to know them and, as relationships developed, I learned of their incredible experiences—experiences unlike anything most of us can even imagine. I also learned that, just like my parents, these refugees and immigrants had come to Canada mainly to secure both an education and a future for their children.

The penny dropped for me one day when I was registering a new student from Afghanistan. "We came so that our children could attend school and have a good life," the child's mother told me through an interpreter. I quickly agreed with her that school was indeed important, although I was referring to school in a general, abstract way. "No," she said forcefully, her voice quaking with emotion as she touched the office wall. "You don't understand. We came for *this* school."

I blinked for a moment as I took this in. Byrne Creek was a new school beset by difficulties, a school the Fraser Institute didn't like any more than Edmonds. And yet this mother had travelled thousands of kilometres to put her most precious possessions—her children—in this school and in my care.

I carried the hopes and expectations of that mother with me to Edmonds Community School two years later when I was offered the position of principal. Edmonds was a very good fit for me. The majority of students at Edmonds

Dave and Nasima Muhammad Aslam, Victor Gonzalez Aguirre, Rifad Bhuyia, Jennifer Mascardo, and Maryam Jawansheer

have siblings at Byrne Creek, and the same district support staff—settlement workers, psychologists, learning support teachers, and the like—service both schools. Although the students are younger at Edmonds, the faces and the names are the same as at the high school, and in many ways the story of Edmonds is incomplete without including the story of Byrne Creek.

Edmonds and Byrne Creek are not easy places to work. In an age of shrinking budgets, the spectre of reduced services hangs constantly over the schools, which have relied on additional staffing and resources from the school district to do their job effectively. In addition, the challenges of working in the inner city—poverty, violence, and drugs—are always present here. The level of commitment demanded of the staff is high; here emotional burn-out is an occupational hazard. But for those who come, stay, and learn to love the students and the neighbourhood, the rewards are extraordinary.

At both Byrne Creek and Edmonds, I've been privileged to be part of a team of educators, counsellors, and community service providers who have dedicated their careers to helping some of Canada's newest and perhaps most vulnerable residents integrate and succeed. The work of these outstanding professionals has become part of the stories of the refugees at these schools, and this book is as much about them as it is about the students and parents.

But always at the heart of the book are the families. This book chronicles their journeys and their experiences and celebrates the roles that Edmonds Community and Byrne Creek Secondary schools have played in educating, acculturating, and welcoming people who have fled from the most dangerous places on earth.

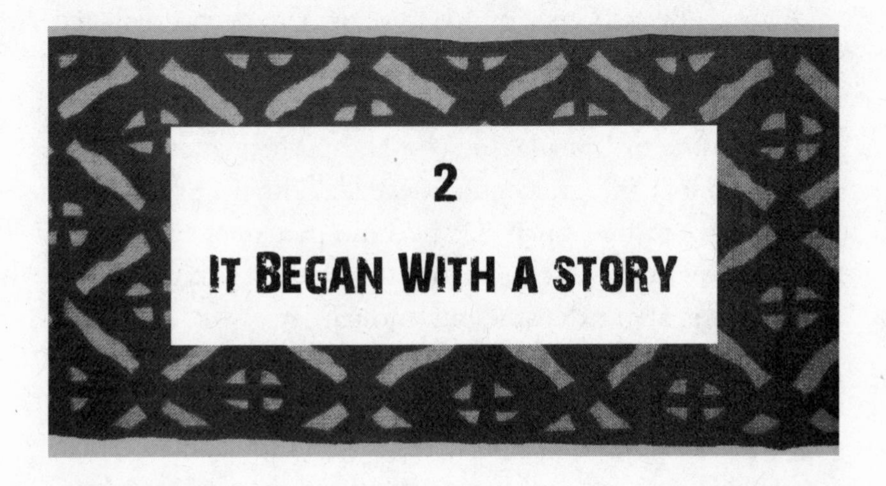

2
It Began With a Story

What the hell am I supposed to do with him?" one of Luc's exasperated teachers asked me a few short weeks into the school year. "The kid's nice enough, but he just won't listen. I tell him to stay in the room, and he just gets up and leaves." I didn't know what to say because, quite frankly, I didn't know what to do with him either. None of us did.

Luc[1] was a seventeen-year-old refugee from the Democratic Republic of Congo. He'd shown up at Byrne Creek Secondary School with his two sisters, been registered, enrolled in his classes, and off he went. But things

[1] The name and other identifying details about this student have been changed. From this point on, an asterisk (*) will be used whenever such changes have been made.

started going sideways for Luc almost immediately. He was an affable young man with short, tightly curled hair, a brilliant smile, and a polite, deferential nature—always saying hello with a handshake and a richly accented "Good morning, sir." The problem was that Luc just simply would not, or could not, follow instructions. He'd arrive for a class, sit for a while, and then slip out, off for a walk through the atrium, stopping to visit friends. As for his work, little, if any, ever made its way back to his teachers and, although there were other students who acted in a similar fashion, Luc became synonymous with the frustration that was building among the staff.

While we were all at a loss over Luc's behaviour, I was the one responsible for figuring it out. It was the fall of 2006 and I had just stepped into the role of vice principal at Byrne Creek Secondary. Situated just ten blocks southwest of Edmonds, my new posting was a study in juxtapositions. Having opened just the year before, Byrne Creek was a brand new architectural showpiece—a gleaming steel-and-glass edifice with wide atriums and a custom-built theatre modelled after the UN General Assembly. The school was also full of the newest technology and amenities, including the teal-coloured fitness equipment from the defunct Vancouver Grizzlies, equipment left behind by the team in its hurried exodus to Memphis. And yet, when the school opened its doors, almost nobody wanted to go to there. Built to relieve over-crowding at two neighbouring high schools, Byrne Creek had a catchment that took in most of the public and low-cost housing projects in the southern half of the city.

Byrne Creek was to be the high school for Edmonds' neighbourhood and the hundreds of refugees who lived there. Because of that demographic, the school suffered a serious image problem well before it opened its doors. Although some people in the neighbourhood were excited about the new school, parents with connections to other high schools were reluctant to send their children to the large concrete building going up on a vacant patch of ugly industrial land across the street from Safeway's BC warehouse and distribution centre. Byrne had no history, no tradition of academic or athletic excellence and, perhaps worst of all, was already labelled as "a low-income, immigrant school" whose hallways were destined to be filled with gangsters and hoodlums.

But Mike Greenway, Byrne Creek's first principal, didn't see it that way. A soft-spoken master principal with decades of experience, Greenway had taken on the enormous task of starting a school from scratch. Lynn Archer, a woman of English stock in her late forties who was highly organized and deeply committed to the experiment that lay ahead, and Chris Sarellas, an easterner from Toronto with a shaved head and an uncanny ability to sound as if he'd been born and bred in New York, joined Greenway as vice principals. This dynamic administrative team oversaw the completion of the construction, hired the school's staff, and shepherded the school through its first crucial year. The first few months were among the most challenging of Greenway's career as he guided the school, helping it develop the friendly and welcoming culture which persists to this day.

At the end of that first year, though, Greenway retired and Sarellas returned to Toronto for family reasons, leaving Lynn Archer to move into the position of principal. I joined her as vice principal along with Ron Hall, a former science teacher and vice principal from Burnaby Central Secondary. Hall, a fisherman who liked nothing better than getting out of the city and casting a fly in a lonely lake, was a passionate sportsman with a long history of coaching soccer. But what I liked best about Hall was the gentle and patient way he had with even the most difficult students. We clicked immediately and were both very happy for the opportunity to work with Archer and the Byrne Creek staff. But we were also well aware that, despite the successes of the first year, some serious issues had emerged that would have to be dealt with as soon as classes began in September.

All schools in every metropolitan region on the continent have ethnic diversity, but the challenge facing Byrne Creek was how to provide a meaningful and effective education for the significant number of students from refugee backgrounds. There had always been refugees at the other Burnaby high schools, but they were small in number and hidden among other immigrants from Asia, Central America, the Middle East, and eastern Europe. At Byrne Creek, however, the sheer number of refugees (slightly more than 15 per cent of the school's population) was almost overwhelming.

It's important to remember that, whether children are from Ethiopia or Edmonton, the ties that bind them together far outnumber their differences. The need to be accepted, fit in, and be loved are universal, as are the desires to own an iPod and wear the newest clothes. Still, refugee students frequently come with needs the average school has difficulty meeting.

Those needs are as varied as the students themselves. A girl from Liberia or Sierra Leone, for example, may speak fluent, albeit heavily accented English, masking the fact that she can't read a word or solve even the most rudimentary mathematical problem. One Afghan boy may be the son of a farmer with no formal education at all, while another is the highly educated son of a professor of archaeology—both boys driven from their homes by the same forces into the same fly-blown refugee camp in Pakistan.

The common thread that connects most refugees—regardless of their cultural, ethnic, and linguistic backgrounds—is that when they arrive at school in North America, they have come from a background of disrupted learning and trauma. Unlike immigrants from places such as South Korea or China, refugees often have never attended classes before, can be illiterate in both their own languages and English, and may be unfamiliar with the discipline and routines of schools.

In my first year at Byrne Creek, all of those challenges were somehow personified by Luc, who was by turns charming and exasperating. For quite a while, we were at a loss to know how to address his behaviour. And then, finally, someone had a brilliant idea. We'd gotten sidetracked, I think, caught up in what this boy was doing and had forgotten all about *who* he was as a human being and why he acted the way he did. We needed to take a step back, give him the chance to introduce himself to staff, let us know what made him tick, and let him tell us his story.

To begin to get to really know Luc, we invited him and several other students to address the teachers at a staff meeting. Luc shyly accepted our invitation, and so we gathered in the library after school—a handful of nervous refugee students and sixty expectant adults—waiting to hear what Luc and the others had to say. Luc took a seat, looked around the room at the faces of his teachers, and spoke.

"When I was a boy," he said slowly, "my mother hid me in a hole under my bed to keep me safe from the soldiers." Whatever sound had been in the room stopped as Luc told his story and, as hackneyed as it sounds, the hair on the back of my neck stood up. All the men and the boys in his remote Congolese village, Luc explained, had been taken—by rebels, government soldiers, whomever—to serve as child soldiers in the interminable war that plagued his country. His father had disappeared, and his mother was not about to let that same fate befall her son.

Luc then described his mother's decision to leave the war-ravaged Congo and seek sanctuary outside of the country. He told us of a trip overland by truck, car, and foot from the Congo to South Africa, where he, his mother, and his sisters led an impoverished existence for several years, during which time they received little, if any, formal education. Eventually they were accepted into Canada as Government Assisted Refugees. They had been in the country just a week or so, he explained, before they'd been settled in the Edmonds neighbourhood and he had enrolled at Byrne Creek.

Luc spoke eloquently, his voice quiet as he told us an amazing story of life, death, hope, and refuge. Some staff members cried as they listened to him. Me? I felt a sense of shame for being frustrated with this boy just because he couldn't sit still in a row and quietly and obediently do his worksheets. Luc thanked us for listening and turned the floor over to another student whose own story was just as powerful. It was at that meeting that I began to understand that the classes we had developed for Luc and others like him were hopelessly inadequate.

We'd been looking at things completely backwards. We'd been trying to make this boy and others like him fit our structures and adjust to our way of doing things when, in fact, it was the system itself that needed to change. I also realized, like a punch in the gut, how important this school was to Luc and his mother, and how much we needed to make damn sure we did everything possible to validate the courage they'd shown and the sacrifices they'd made just to reach our doors.

It began with a story—a simple, powerful story told by a student about what he had endured. As I looked around the halls of the school in the days that followed and talked to the students with backgrounds similar to Luc's, I found myself wondering what their stories were, what they'd been through, and what prices they had paid to come here. And not just the students already enrolled. There were more coming, from Rwanda, Iraq, and a host of other places. Today, more than ever in our increasingly unstable world, geopolitical tsunamis inundate countries like the Democratic Republic of the Congo, Afghanistan, and Sudan with famine, war, and genocide—and the survivors from these tumultuous events wash up at the doorstep of Byrne Creek Secondary and Edmonds Community School; survivors like Lois Arop.

3
We Can Overcome Anything

Lois Arop is a Grade 7 student at Edmonds Community School. She is a beautiful, tall young woman with corn-row hair, an incredible smile, a gift for learning languages, and a talent for driving her teachers to their wits' end. Her time in Canada has not been without struggles, and she has found herself frequently in my office, debriefing one problem or another. "I'm flabbergasted about it myself," she said recently after being sent down to the office, although the smile on her face indicated that she knew exactly what she'd done. A quick investigation concluded that Lois had gotten off lightly, and all her teacher really needed was a well-deserved break from the girl.

Amel Madut and Nyiwer Chol

There is much to like about Lois. She can be disruptive and cause no end of mischief when she sets her mind to it, but her heart is good and there is no one in the school better suited to being assigned an important job or helping out with the kindergarten children at lunchtime. Currently Lois's thoughts are on learning sign language and Japanese, and perhaps going to live in Boston with one of her mother's sisters. She is also thinking of changing her name from Lois Adthel, a family name to honour her Sudanese roots.

Lois's roots are, to say the least, complex: they have fed on both the best and the worst of humanity and have grown with resiliency, love, and determination. I have been entrusted with the story of those roots, a story that not only enlightened me about Lois and her many siblings and cousins, but also deepened my understanding of the courage, faith, and determination that brought them into my world.

I learn about the journey that brought Lois's family to Edmonds from Amel Madut and Nyiwer Chol, cousins by birth who call themselves "sisters in struggle." Amel, Lois's mother, is tall and slender like her Dinka ancestors. Nyiwer is just as striking, but where Amel's face is angular and spare, hers is rounder, almost always smiling, and neatly framed by short-cropped hair. Between them, they have eleven children. Some were born in this country, while others shared the journey out of Africa with their mothers. Several of their children still attend Edmonds or Byrne Creek. Although I've spent considerable time with their sons and daughters over the years, it is Amel and Nyiwer, my friends for five years now, who sit in my office today.

The door is closed, and the women look nervously at the tape recorder on the table, about to share things rarely—if ever—spoken of outside the family. But theirs is an important story, and they both want to share it. After all, they have done more than study the tragic recent history of their country; they have been an integral part of it.

Amel and Nyiwer were born in 1970 in the Sahel city of Rumbek, the capital of the southern Sudanese province of Al Buhayrat. Life for them was, by Sudanese standards, both pleasant and privileged. "We had a happy childhood," Nyiwer begins. "We used to play together, go to school together, and go to church together. We were like sisters, and I had it particularly good. I was the only girl in my house, and my father loved me very much. I was also the talkative one while Amel was quiet. It was always like that."

That dynamic holds true today. It is Nyiwer who speaks more than her cousin, though she does stop her narrative frequently to confer with Amel on matters of dates, events, and names, deferring often to her quieter cousin's memory. "Rumbek was a good place to grow up," Amel agrees, "a place of green in the wet season and heat in the dry. You may not realize it, but we would have much rain in South Sudan from March through to September, and it would pool on the streets and on the flat landscape and capture the reflection of the sky above. In Sudan, water is life, you know, but it is also a mixed blessing because water was where the hippos and the crocodiles lived, and I was taught to be very careful around it."

Both girls were taught many things. Although it was not the case for all Sudanese children, education was greatly valued by their parents and it played a key role in their lives. "My father, Madut, was an educated man, a man of prominence," says Amel proudly. "He was a director of education in the city and both he and my mother, Yar, made certain that the five boys and three girls in our family attended school."

Nyiwer's parents shared a similar view. "My father, David, was a very educated man as well, a doctor of veterinary medicine, and he sent me to school when I was six years old. We were good children, and Amel and I were never in trouble. The teachers were happy with us, our parents were happy with us, we got good grades, and we liked school very much. Which was a good thing," she adds, "because in Rumbek the teachers would beat you until you learned to like their classes."

As much as the girls enjoyed school, the education system was symptomatic of the great divide that existed in Sudan, a rift that separated the country into north and south, Arabic and Black, Muslim and Christian. "We were Dinka but we were forced to be educated in Arabic," explains Amel. "And the national curriculum included studying the Qur'an, even though we weren't Muslim. We were told by our teachers that school was for the Qur'an while church was for the Bible. Even though I was just a child, as a Christian I had problems with this arrangement. I didn't like learning the Qur'an and I didn't like what the northerners were doing to us. I felt like we were being kept down, like we were being kept in ignorance and dominated by Khartoum and by the Arabs who travelled down the Nile to take over our businesses and our land. The word *Sudan* means, after all, 'land of the Black people,' but we didn't feel like it was our own country, not in the least."

Domination by the Arab north has always been of great concern to southerners, so much so that the two halves of Sudan have been at war with each other intermittently since independence in 1956, though the roots of the conflict stretch much further back, to the British colonial takeover of 1885. The British split the Sudan into two—the predominantly Arabic and Islamic north and the Dinka and English-speaking Christian south—and for the next four decades treated the disparate regions of the Sudan, each full of enmity and suspicion of the other, as separate entities. After the Second World War, however, Sudan was hastily reunited in a marriage of convenience by a tired, broken, and exhausted Britain, anxious to get out of Africa and the colonial game at all costs. Independence was declared and, in a pattern quite common in Africa, civil war broke out soon after—a war that would rage for a decade until a peace accord that gave the south partial self-government was signed in 1972.

That uneasy peace would shatter in 1983, the year Amel and Nyiwer turned thirteen. "Our fathers knew politics, were politically active, and mine was even a politician himself once," Nyiwer says. "They would always talk about what was going on in the south. We were all very aware and knew about the problems in our country." Chief among the problems faced by the south Sudanese was the imposition of Sharia, Islamic religious law, on the entire country—a move made especially galling since it followed, by just a few years, the discovery of massive reserves of oil in the southern half of the country. For many, this timely clampdown by Khartoum was more than just coincidence, and for some it was the final straw.

In 1983 the Sudan People's Liberation Movement and its military arm, the Sudanese People's Liberation Army, were formed to protect the autonomy, culture, religious beliefs, and economy of the south Sudan. Led by John Garang, a Dinka man educated in the United States and Tanzania, the SPLA was prepared to spill blood and eagerly took up arms against the government.

Amel recalls very clearly the morning bullets started flying on the streets of Rumbek. "We were in class when we heard shots and people shouting and screaming." She describes a scene of chaos as the students attempted to flee their school and run home to the protection of their parents. The teachers, looking out on streets now red with blood, blocked the doors of the school with their bodies and sheltered the children from the government troops who roamed outside, shooting indiscriminately at whoever crossed their paths. "When things quieted down and the army left," continued Nyiwer, "the teachers let us out and we quickly went home. But, from that time on, we didn't leave our houses after dark. We learned that if the soldiers saw you, they'd take you away and you would disappear in the night."

In May 1984, the violence returned after a short truce. "It was a pleasant day," recalls Nyiwer. "We were at our school when, at about two in the afternoon, the gunfire erupted. This time the teachers couldn't save us. There were too many men with guns and so we ran. We wanted to go home, but the soldiers were in the streets shooting women, children, everyone. They were blocking our way home and to stay put was to die, so we ran the opposite way, to the edge of town."

More than twenty-five years after the attack on Rumbek, Amel and Nyiwer still shake at the memory. "That first night in the bush was very bad," says Amel. "We met other children and students hiding there as well. Some were our age and some were older, but most of the others were much younger than us—eight, nine years old maybe. We were all very scared. We cried, and we wanted our parents, and then these men with guns found us. At first we thought that maybe we'd been captured by government soldiers, but these men were SPLA rebels and they stayed with us, protected us, and gave us blankets and mosquito nets. We rested for a while and then they collected us up and we started to walk. It wasn't as if they made us go with them, but what else could we do?" says Amel. "Stay in Rumbek? Get raped by the government soldiers? Besides, we thought everyone we loved had been killed and so we went." For Amel, Nyiwer, and tens of thousands of other Sudanese children, including the ones most famously known as The Lost Boys, this was how their walk would begin, a walk that would take them across three countries and would test the very limits of human endurance and suffering. "We didn't know where we were going, we just travelled and cried for hours," explains Nyiwer. "We would stop for thirty minutes to rest occasionally until the rebels would order us to pick up whatever things we had and keep walking. They explained to us that this was the second *Anyanya*, the second civil war against the government, and we were caught up in it."

"From May to August of 1984 we just walked," says Amel flatly. "There were maybe three hundred of us children, and we walked, day and night, never knowing where we were going. When we came near a village, the rebel soldiers would approach the chief and ask for food for us and normally, though not always, they would provide us with maize, peanuts, and other food and water. The villagers would also tell us where to go, or perhaps where not to go next. South Sudan is a dangerous place and they would warn us where the lions or the soldiers were waiting."

One day the rebel leader in charge of the group announced that he'd decided to take the children to Ethiopia, to the refugee camps for displaced Sudanese that had been established by the UN and a government in Addis Ababa sympathetic to the plight of the southerners. Amel and Nyiwer finally knew their destination: now all they had to do was survive a one-thousand-kilometre trek through scrub and desert, hide from the Sudanese armed forces, avoid being killed by wildlife, and cross two rivers without drowning.

"What else could we do?" asks Nyiwer, "and so we walked. For many days of that journey we couldn't see houses or towns, just the bush and the desert. Almost every living thing out there—rhinos, lions, snakes, everything—could harm you. We had no water and no food for up to three days and so we'd take cloth and cinch it tightly around our waists to ease the pains of hunger. Sometimes, if we were lucky, we would eat the fruit we found on the trees, but we were always thirsty, so thirsty. We'd drink our own urine and sometimes we would come across these pools of stagnant rainwater. It wasn't good and we knew it, but we'd do anything to have liquid and so we drank through our shirts to filter the water and to keep the leeches and the frogs from our throats."

The children, now dressed in rags, were starving and suffering from a host of diseases, but of all the horrors they faced, the worst came from above. "Sometimes the military would get information from the villagers who had helped us," says Amel without animosity, knowing full well the fate of those who refused to help the army. And with that intelligence, military aircraft flew high above the brown landscape searching for the ragged columns of children that snaked their way east to the Ethiopian border, children the Sudanese government had vowed never to let escape.

"The worst were the bombers," Amel remembers. "We would hide in the day and travel by night because we were too visible in daylight. Also, we could never light cooking fires even if we had food because at day the smoke would give away our position and at night the flames would."

"The most terrifying sound of all was the roar of the engines approaching overhead," continues Nyiwer. "And running was the worst. They'd see you for sure and those who ran died. You learned quickly that if you heard that sound you didn't move. After all, if a bomb fell on you there was nothing you could do. It was your day. You were done." Her voice drops to a whisper as the words and the memories flow. "So many of us died along the way," she says sadly. "So many."

Some months after leaving Rumbek, the children reached the town of Bor, a key location in the conflict. It was in Bor that John Garang, then a lieutenant-colonel in the Sudanese army, had been tasked with crushing an army mutiny but had instead chosen to found the SPLA and take up arms against his own government. And it would again be in Bor, eight years after Nyiwer and Amel passed through it, that one of the worst atrocities in Sudanese history occurred. Thousands of people, mostly Dinka women and children, were massacred, not at the hands of the government but by a breakaway faction of the SPLA itself.

The most striking physical landmark of Bor is the Nile and, although the river was a beautiful sight after weeks in the desert, the muddy expanse of water and marshland presented a daunting obstacle for the children and their rebel protectors. The crossing, Amel remembers, was a harrowing experience: "The soldiers were looking for us, there was no bridge we could cross, no ferry we could take, and crocodiles were in the water, so the people who lived there ferried us across the river in crude canoes. We were crammed naked together, and we couldn't move for the six hours or so it took us to cross the river and go through the marshes."

Safe on the other side of the river, they continued to walk. By late summer, after months of travel, the remnants of the pitiful convoy of children reached the Ethiopian border near the Sudanese town of Nasir. Now all that stood between them and the protection of the refugee camp was the crossing of another river, this time the Baro, not nearly as wide as the Nile but still a formidable obstacle. "That day the army was waiting," says Amel. "We were told the rebels had shot down some Sudanese government planes, and the soldiers were angry. They knew we were coming and looked to take out their frustration on us."

"In that part of the Sudan, the villagers were always naked around the water," adds Nyiwer, "but some of us still had clothes and clothes meant you were a city person, and so we stripped, stood naked on the banks and pretended to be locals." There would be no canoes to aid in the crossing this time. If the children and their protectors wanted to reach Ethiopia, they would have to swim. "Those who could swim did so, but we didn't know how, and so we held onto sticks and were swum across by others. Before we got into the river, Amel and I said to each other that if we were going to die at this place then we'd die together, so we held onto the same stick, jumped into the water, and let the men take us toward the far bank. We didn't breathe, we didn't think. All we could do was kick our legs. I remember a boy beside us panicking. He nearly drowned the man helping him swim across, so the man took the boy's head, shoved it under the water, pulled him up a few seconds later, and said the next time he did that he'd put him underwater again and not pull him back up."

Through some miracle both cousins made it across the river, but when they reached the far bank they quickly realized that they were among the lucky few. Of the estimated 300 children who'd started the journey from Rumbek with them, hardly sixty remained, according to Amel and Nyiwer.

Many had been shot by soldiers, while others had been killed by falling bombs, thirst, hunger, or illness along the way. Some died from the venomous snakes that dropped silently upon them from the trees, or from the lions and other predators that hid along the paths and jumped upon stragglers, dragging them away screaming. But the most unlucky of children drowned in the Baro River or disappeared in a seething mass of water, ambushed by crocodiles, within sight of sanctuary.

The survivors were quickly apprehended by Ethiopian authorities and transferred to the Itang refugee camp, one of the largest in the world at the time. In those years, the regime of Ethiopian President Mengistu Haile Mariam was friendly to the flood of Sudanese refugees that crossed into his country. He was so friendly in fact that Itang and other refugee camps in Ethiopia were used freely by Garang and the SPLA as both a base and a source of new recruits. Young boys would frequently be taken, given rudimentary military training and guns, and then would slip back across the border, back into Sudan to carry on the SPLA's war.

In the fall of 1984, Nyiwer and Amel were now safe from the Sudanese army. However, they were still very much prisoners of both the politics and culture of their homeland and the camp itself. Not long after arriving in Itang, the fourteen-year-old cousins—like many other orphaned and displaced refugee girls and women—were quickly taken as brides by soldiers of the SPLA and would both soon be pregnant. "A Sudanese woman's job is to get married and have children," Amel says. "Often there is no love, no nothing, but what can you do? You have to live, you know? If you are a woman you have no choice."

Nyiwer nods in agreement. "Our husbands were soldiers and would leave us alone in the camps and go to war. Those were very difficult times for sure, and I sometimes wonder how we managed to come out of this alive." The women had been ripped from their families, survived a horrendous march across Sudan, and endured marriages forced upon them, but life was made bearable by the fact they had each other. Then one day in 1987, even that small comfort was taken from them when Amel's husband took her from Itang to Dimma, another refugee camp, on SPLA business.

With the exception of a brief period in 1993, when they found themselves together in a refugee camp in Kenya, Amel and Nyiwer were separated for eighteen tumultuous years. For Nyiwer, those years felt like a lifetime—a lifetime of dust and heat and flies, of lining up every day for their small allotments of food and oil and water, of trying to keep her sick and hungry children alive, of fleeing bombs and snipers with a three-year-old son and an eight-day-old baby in tow. During that time, she lost the husband whom she had come to love and found herself in the tenuous role of widow. In a desperate search for safety, she crossed Tanzania, Malawi, Mozambique, South Africa, and Zimbabwe. For Amel, most of those eighteen years were spent either at Kakuma refugee camp in Kenya or in the capital, Nairobi, where she found work as a translator through the help of a UN worker sympathetic to her plight. Suffering physical and emotional abuse at the hands of her husband and in-laws, she was desperately trying to find security and independence, despite the escalating violence in the world around her.

As I listened to Amel and Nyiwer's stories, it was difficult not lament the loss of the two innocent young cousins who had happily studied together, had loved and been loved by their families, and had believed that the world was a gift of beauty and endless possibilities. And yet, as I looked into the faces of the two women sitting across from me, I was overwhelmed by a sense of the power of the human spirit and humbled by the extraordinary courage which they embodied.

Unbeknownst to each other, both Amel and Nyiwer managed to find their way through the difficult process of being accepted as refugees and of moving to Canada. Amel arrived in Vancouver in 2003 and soon settled in the Edmonds neighbourhood, found an apartment, and quickly enrolled her children—Victor, Priscilla, and Lois—into Edmonds Community School. Two years later—twenty-one years after the day when they lost all sense of home, family, and security—Nyiwer, her second husband Michael, and her children made their own move to Canada and safety.

When refugees arrive in Vancouver, their first stop is usually Welcome House, a downtown facility that provides approximately one hundred beds in self-contained one- and two-bedroom apartments, and office space for the team of counsellors and other workers who provide comfort and assistance to people who have sometimes made the tumultuous transition from refugee camp to Canada in as little as forty-eight hours. It is at the heart of Immigrant Services Society of British Columbia (ISS), an organization that provides settlement, language, and career services. And so, when Amel learned of her cousin's impending arrival, she went to Welcome House to wait for her.

"That day I smiled from morning till night," says Nyiwer. "It was a good day. And I loved Welcome House as well. It was a place of peace and the people there really cared about me. And I had a bed. For years I could hardly imagine a blanket, let alone a bed. At Welcome House there was also medical care and there was no meningitis, no malaria, no disease, no hunger, and no war."

Nyiwer found a place not far from Amel's apartment and sent her own children—Charles and Susan—to Byrne Creek Secondary. During her first few weeks in Canada, Nyiwer, like Amel before her, quickly discovered that life in Canada was not going to be as simple as she'd hoped. Like all Government Assisted Refugees in Canada, they were expected to pay back, with interest, the cost of the plane tickets that had been purchased for them and their families. For Nyiwer, Michael, and their children, that bill was more than $8,000.

As the months and years in Canada passed, both women adjusted to their new lives with a mixture of gratitude, sadness and, at times, resentment. "Canada's such a beautiful place," says Amel, "but after Kenya I found it a little boring. My mom had joined us in Nairobi and there our house was busy, always full of laughing, always full of family, but here even with my cousin I feel alone. I guess you just have to get on with things."

For Amel, "getting on with things" meant taking a menial job cleaning an office building downtown, doing whatever she could to support her children. "I can't help thinking that maybe if we'd gone straight to Canada from Sudan I could have been a doctor by now. I once had dreams of going to school, but there I was in that building, scrubbing the toilets and crying. I had difficulty telling my mother what I was doing here for work, but still I was happy to come to this country so that my children would get an education."

Amel has had two more children since her arrival in Canada. Her son, six-year-old Bobby, a quiet and introspective child, is at Edmonds in a Grade 1/2 class. The youngest, Junior, manages to spend considerable time at the school with his mother and siblings, even though he is three years away from kindergarten. Nyiwer's daughter, Susan, graduated from Byrne Creek Secondary with very good marks and is currently attending university, although Nyiwer worries she may have to quit because the tuition is so expensive. Victor and Charles, on the other hand, left high school a few courses short of their diplomas and are, according to Amel and Nyiwer, "still trying to figure things out," much to their mothers' chagrin. "I worry that Victor didn't focus enough on his future or his education," Amel admits. "You want your children to appreciate their freedom and not take it for granted."

But Amel and Nyiwer are cautiously optimistic that Victor, Charles, and other young refugee men like them will come around and find a direction and focus. Both women realize that, even with the frustration and uncertainty they still face, they are far luckier than most. "This is the land of opportunity," Amel says, "and with help and support you can succeed."

For Amel's daughter, Lois, success most definitely is within reach—although, like many young women her age, she still has her doubts and traumas.

"I hate this place," she told me one day while running off a long list of reasons why she felt that way. Topping her grievances was the complaint that she didn't feel listened to or respected. "It was different in Africa," she added, her voice softening. "It was better there in some ways too, you know." I asked her what she meant and, though she was young when she left Kenya, Lois vividly described the heat of a Nairobi afternoon playing happily with her family in Uhuru Park. As we sat and did math questions together, she poignantly articulated the heart of the problem, as far as she was concerned. "Our family is spread out now," she said. "Seattle, Boston, back in Sudan. Sometimes I feel halfway between places and cut off from my history, you know?"

"But there are good things about here as well, don't you think?" I asked.

"Sure." she said. "Soccer. Dance. Music. And track."

Like many of Edmonds' students, Lois is very good at track. Shortly after our conversation, Lois ran in an invitational tournament in Richmond and won a medal in her race. When we walked proudly back to the bus at the end of the day, with Lois carrying the trophy for overall meet winner, the smile on her face assured me that she believes success is possible.

Lois's aunt, Nyiwer, puts it all in perspective: "When you step into this country, you can't come here thinking you will become rich—but you can be successful. People have to believe, have to really believe that they can achieve their dreams. As refugees, we need to work hard and always remember that we can become anything we want. One day we will. We want people to know that suffering shapes a person to become better. A struggle can make you strong, and we know that if we can overcome the things we experienced, we can overcome anything."

Lois Arop

4

THIS PLACE FEEDS MY SOUL

The freshly waxed hallways of Edmonds Community School were a stark place without the sound of the students, and the school had an empty, hollow feel about it. Dino Klarich, the school's new vice principal, and I should have been in the office getting ready for the upcoming school year, but our custodians had just steam-cleaned the carpet and had asked politely if we'd mind going out for an hour or so to let it dry.

It was a hot day in late August, so we eagerly took the opportunity to go outside and enjoy the sun. "Let's go for a walk," I suggested. "This might be a good opportunity to get you out into the community and get a sense of the neighbourhood."

"It would be nice to meet some of the kids," Dino agreed, and so we cut across the gravel field, dry and dusty in the heat, got to Edmonds Street, and headed west, past Fire Hall 2, the Little Cockatoo restaurant, Cony's African Market, the Dollar Store, and the bottle depot. Dino had worked in Burnaby for nearly twenty years, but he was a North Burnaby boy, and Edmonds was a very different place from the comfortable middle-class neighbourhoods to the north. "Where are we going?" he asked as we turned south on Mary and made a quick right on 18th Avenue.

"To where most of our students live," I replied. "We're going to Hillside Gardens."

Hillside Gardens is a sprawling complex of low-rise apartment buildings at the corner of 18th and Kingsway. Now government-subsidized and well managed, Hillside has made significant improvements over the years, but the complex has long struggled to overcome the reputation of being a substandard place to live—the sort of place where only the poorest and most desperate of people choose to reside. Hillside is also home to a significant number of the children who attend Edmonds Community School. If Dino wanted to meet Edmonds' students, there was no better place to start.

We walked into the courtyard of the complex and were greeted by the scent of spicy food, Afghan music blaring from an open window, and a handful of children playing in the open space. They quickly ran over to say hello and, as if through telepathy, our presence became quickly known. Soon two dozen or so familiar faces gathered around us as we stood next to the small pool that in three years I'd never seen full of water. The kids were happy to see me, and they asked how my summer had been, but the main target of inquiry was Dino.

"He's the new guy, right Mr. Starr?" one of them asked. I nodded in confirmation, and soon Dino was peppered by questions. Within just a few minutes his skilful interrogators had gleaned a substantial amount of information from their new vice principal, probably far more than he'd planned on sharing. He also did a commendable job remembering names, as the kids rapidly introduced themselves—Bukar, Nasri, Sufi, Abdul, Mohammed, Milad, Shabnam, Maryam, and a score more—names substantially more exotic than those from his previous school with its 100 or so suburban students, only a five-minute drive but a world away from Hillside Gardens.

We spent about thirty minutes at Hillside and, after saying goodbye and reminding students what day school started, we took our leave, carried on our walk, and went back to the school where a substantial pile of paperwork and a beautifully cleaned carpet waited for us. It was a very good visit and one that paid many dividends. When the kids came in for their first day, almost every single student in the school knew Dino's name and knew that he'd gone to Hillside to see them because he thought they were important.

My own first day at Edmonds had been three years earlier. Having spent almost all of my thirteen years in education at the middle or secondary level, it was my first foray into an elementary school. For me, the most intimidating thing about becoming principal at Edmonds was the size and age of the students. I was used to working with eighteen year olds—students who were more adult than child—and the size and energy of the little people who swarmed around my

Vice principal Dino Klarich

legs quite frankly scared the hell out of me. And they were so *touchy*, wanting hugs, pulling on arms and hands. This wasn't something that occurred with Grade 12 students. One of the teachers walked past me and smiled. She seemed friendly enough, but I knew what that look really meant. *Good luck, pal*, she was saying. *You have no idea what you're in for*.

But I thought I did. For the past two years I'd been the vice principal at Byrne Creek and had worked with the older siblings of the children at Edmonds. I knew many of the parents and the board's itinerant workers (the district psychologist, the settlement workers who serviced newcomers to the Edmonds neighbourhood, and so on). I'd met and worked with Al Post, the outgoing principal, on many occasions and knew both Stephanie Miller, the vice principal at the time, and Elin Horton, the head teacher.

In fact, the degree of overlap between Byrne and Edmonds was substantial and deceivingly comfortable. I knew families, recognized faces, and perhaps most important of all, thought I'd gained an understanding of the unique needs of a school where nearly one-third of the children were from refugee backgrounds. Edmonds would not be an easy place to work. I knew that going in. But this was an assignment I'd asked for, and I thought that I was more than prepared. Looking back, however, I think that perhaps that teacher who'd smiled at me was right after all. I really didn't have a clue what I was getting myself into. But that's the way it goes at Edmonds, a place where every new teacher's first days are full of surprises.

Elin Horton nearly didn't survive her own first week at Edmonds. In her mid-fifties, of sturdy Viking stock, with a dominant personality, flame-red hair, and a well-practiced don't-mess-with-me look, Elin was Edmonds' learning resource teacher for many years. She developed learning plans, worked one-on-one with struggling students, and passionately advocated for students with severe physical, mental, and emotional challenges. She was also the school's head teacher, a key administrative support position with a range of duties, such as scheduling gym times, organizing assemblies, and ensuring that the supply of basketballs and photocopy paper never runs out. A confident and hard-working teacher, she was the living soul of the building. Sixteen years ago, however, she had a rude awakening when she first walked through the doors.

"I started working at Edmonds Community School in 1996," she said, "fifteen years or so into my teaching career.

I came for an interview and I felt the heartbeat and the vibe of the place and I thought *Yeah, this is where I want to be*. I got hired and took up my first job at the school, a half learning-assistant and half kindergarten-teacher position. There's no other place like this in the city," she added, "and refugees have been part of the fabric of this school as long as I've been here—Bosnians and Croats at height of the Balkan war, the Afghans starting around 2000, and now the Africans and Mexicans—but no matter where they're from, these students and their families bring with them certain things.

"The negatives include trauma, poverty, no initial point of connection to their new home and, for some, no previous experience of school. Ever. However, what they have in common is something so powerful it can overcome all the bad—and that's hope. They have such tremendous hope, and our job is to help them realize it."

The students very nearly overwhelmed Elin at the beginning. "I had these twenty-seven kids in my kindergarten class and, oh my God! There were these twins, one of whom was a voracious learner, but the other? All he did was cry all the time, and nobody knew why. There was this girl who refused to leave the room and had to be carried out every time we went somewhere. There was also a boy with fetal alcohol syndrome and another girl who'd been apprehended by social services when she was a year and a half and had only just been reunited with her parents. And then there were the rest—mostly refugees or immigrants—and hardly any of them spoke English. It was like nothing I could ever have imagined."

Over time, Elin learned first-hand how special—and how challenging—the children in the building could be. "It's about equity," she explained. "Our job is to ensure equity for all kids. It's not about giving every student the same thing, but rather giving all children what they need to achieve the same outcome. Many children are blessed with resources outside of the school, but most of ours are not and it's our job to see that, despite poverty, they have the same chances as any other child at a successful life."

Elin was the first to admit there were many times she considered leaving Edmonds and moving on to an easier, less challenging environment. "I remember at the end of my first week stepping out into the hallway to catch my breath. I mean, I had no idea how hard it would be. And then I saw this veteran teacher from Edmonds, Linda Haynes, and she looked at me and smiled and gave me a this-is-normal-and-you're-going-to-be-okay look and I smiled back and went back to the class. The first days are the hardest and, though there have been plenty more moments like that, this place feeds my soul and I could never leave." Her willingness to stay was a very fortunate thing indeed for the Aguirre family—desperate refugee claimants from Mexico who arrived at the school in 2005. But it is the family—not Elin—who fills me in on the significant role Elin played in their extraordinary story.

When I get together with Sonia Aguirre, she is recovering from a recent gall bladder operation. Sitting is uncomfortable for her and, each time she winces in pain, her son Fernando strokes her hand and wears her discomfort as if it was his own. Fernando has his mother's dark eyes, small frame, and sensitive soul and, as he cuddles her protectively on the couch of their pristine apartment, his love for his mother is palpable. Although he is a slight boy and short for his age, Fernando seems infinitely older than his ten

Head teacher Elin Horton

years would suggest. The younger of Sonia's two children, Fernando has always been close to his mother, both physically and emotionally. It comes as no surprise to me that he offered—insisted really—to help his mother translate, although her own English was more than up to the task.

Sonia's older son, twelve-year-old Victor, loves her just as much, but he's back at the school with other things on his mind. A volleyball game to watch and "some girl problems," he explains confidentially, "but nothing I can't handle."

The Aguirre apartment is prime real estate—a two-bedroom place in the new wing of Hillside Gardens. Sonia Aguirre is a well-educated woman, trained in human resources, although she became a stay-at-home mother after Victor's birth. When asked why they would leave their country and seek asylum in the north, Sonia's eyes welled with tears.

"We didn't want to. It was a good life back home and I loved Mexico—it is a beautiful place. But there were some problems—big problems. Political issues with my father," she explains reluctantly. "He was always the sort of man to fight for little people, the kind to lead protests and to stand up for something when no one else would. But in Mexico, that comes at a cost."

The cost of her father's political activism was a series of assaults, jail sentences, and death threats—common occurrences, she says, in a corrupt and violent Mexico, a place where making enemies of politically connected people is dangerous and often results in kidnapping or assassination. But even though they were not involved in her father's politics, there also were consequences for Sonia and her family. There are many ways to hurt a man who makes problems in Mexico; targeting his family is often used when a strong message needs to be sent. In 2005, someone sent Sonia's father such a message.

"To hurt my father, we were threatened with death as well. Me, my children, all of us. After that, I knew it wasn't safe in Mexico anymore," says Sonia. "My father himself refused to go with us, but said he understood why we'd feel unsafe. My husband had family in Vancouver and so we packed our things and left without telling anyone. We were very quiet and we were very quick." Her husband, Victor Sr., came first, secured a place to stay, and six weeks later sent for Sonia and his children. In July 2005, they followed him north.

"I'll never forget landing in Vancouver," Fernando says. "We were all wearing these big jackets because we thought it would be cold in Canada—Yukon cold!" he laughs. "And then we got outside and found out that it was hot and sunny just like it was in Mexico." Reunited in Vancouver, the family traveled to a citizenship and immigration office and claimed refugee status, setting in motion a process that would dominate the next three years of their lives and almost overwhelm them.

The United Nations High Commissioner for Refugees, and the countries that signed onto the 1951 convention, recognize several different categories of refugee. The first of these are Government Assisted Refugees, people whom the UN recognizes as urgently needing protection and whom our government is willing to accept *en masse.* GARs are given Permanent Resident status upon arrival in Canada, are supported monetarily for one year, and are immediately entitled to health care and education. Other categories of refugees are those who are accepted either under the Joint Assistance Program (that is, they are co-sponsored through a partnership of the government and private groups such as churches) or who are privately sponsored (often by family members who promise to support them for a minimum of one year and pay the costs associated for resettlement).

None of these categories applied to the Aguirre family. Instead, they found themselves in the most tenuous of situations, that of a refugee claimant. A great deal of publicity, most of it negative, has been focused in recent years on refugee claimants: people who have reached Canada legally or otherwise and then claim asylum upon arrival. Well-documented recent refugee cases include a mask-wearing Chinese national, a ship carrying Tamils from Sri Lanka, and a certain Hollywood movie star and his wife. Spurious or not, all claimants have their cases adjudicated by the Immigration and Refugee Board of Canada and must wait, often for months or even years, for a decision.

The Aguirre family's case was doubtful from the start—but not for lack of legitimacy. Canada does not look kindly upon Mexicans applying for refugee status. Mexico is both a neighbour and an economic partner, and despite the scourges of drug-fuelled violence and poverty, the Canadian government does not regard Mexicans as people generally needing protection. A family whose children attended Edmonds Community School was recently deported back to Mexico, and these facts were foremost in the minds of the Victor and Sonia Aguirre when they presented themselves at immigration.

"We spoke to this lady who was standing at the reception window of the office, and she took our names and address," explains Sonia. "She didn't ask why we were claiming refugee status or anything, just took the information and gave us an appointment to speak with an official. When the time came for this meeting, we returned. There was a Spanish interpreter present, and we were told to explain why it was that we had to leave Mexico. This man then arranged for another appointment with another official who would listen to our claim to determine whether or not we had a good chance to stay in Canada," Sonia says. "So we returned for another meeting and then we were told that our situation was eligible to be heard, but that we'd need a lot of proof about what we said because our situation was based, in large part, on my father's troubles—and he'd refused to leave Mexico."

With temporary status in the country assured, Sonia's husband Victor applied for a work permit but, like so many other immigrant and refugee professionals in this country, he quickly found out that he was unable to find work in his profession as a petroleum engineer. So, with children to feed, he took a job as a janitor at a shopping mall until he found better work in construction. "This was very difficult for my husband," Sonia admits. "He felt sad—he still feels sad that, as a skilled worker, he is not able to get a job in his area."

"My dad has such long days," Fernando adds. "He's often gone by five in the morning and usually doesn't come home until six or seven at night." But Victor wasn't the only member of the family to have to work. Desperate to earn enough money to provide food and a decent place for their children to live, and with both boys accepted at school, Sonia returned to the workforce herself and took a job cleaning bathrooms in an office building. And there were other costs to carry as well. They needed to retain the assistance of an immigration lawyer to help them with their claim, and this service didn't come cheap.

The money invested in legal help did not seem to pay off when, several months after their initial application for asylum, word came back from the federal government that their claim had been denied. "This official said he didn't believe us, didn't believe our story," she says, "and I was so sad and depressed. We were all scared and frightened and our lawyer was upset as well because he believed that we had a very good case."

Claimants do not have the right to appeal decisions made by the Canadian Immigration and Refugee Board. There is, however, the option of asking for a review to see if any errors occurred or if pertinent information was not taken into consideration. So that was the course the Aguirre family took next. They prayed, put their hope and trust in their lawyer, and waited. "Six months later," Sonia says, "the answer came back and it was no again, and we were told we had to go. We were devastated, and we talked about what would happen when we went back. My husband promised he would find us a safe place, but I got so depressed I needed help and so I went to see a counsellor. What happened, though, was that old wounds opened up instead. When I was a child, you see, I was abused and, instead of talking about the stress from the case, I found that this was the place I went to. The old hurt never goes away, I suppose. It will always find a way to come out."

"It was so hard on us that time," concurs Fernando. "Me and Victor were young and our parents didn't tell us at the time that the answer was no, but I could see their stress and I knew something was wrong. I call that time the Dark Ages."

During their personal Dark Ages, the Aguirre family was supported by Elin Horton. Elin's connections to the families at Edmonds went far beyond her job description. With the Aguirre family, Elin's support ranged from helping Sonia pay for an unexpected ambulance ride to the hospital when Fernando got hurt, to getting both the provincial MLA for Burnaby-Edmonds and the federal MP involved in the family's case.

For sixteen years, Elin was Edmonds' conscience—leading by example and bringing hope to the children and families she worked with. By 2007 hope was rapidly running out for Aguirre family. Citizenship and Immigration Canada allows, on very rare occasions, for unsuccessful refugee claimants to stay in Canada on "humanitarian and compassionate grounds." Elin encouraged the family to hold on to hope and try this last-available recourse.

Knowing the odds but with nothing left to lose, the Aguirres instructed their lawyer to proceed. "We knew the only option left open for us was to apply, to beg to stay on compassionate grounds," Sonia explains. "This was our last chance and so we applied. But then we didn't hear from the government. For nearly a year and a half—nothing. Not a word. Then, one day in the spring of 2009, I got a call from my husband. He said he had news about our case but that he didn't want to tell me on the phone. He would meet me at Save-On-Foods and tell me there."

The trip to the grocery store was, Sonia remembers, one of the most agonizing journeys of her life. She was absolutely convinced their final appeal had failed and that her husband wanted her to tell her in public so she wouldn't do something rash when he broke the bad news. But what happened next was something she had not dared hope for. "When I got there I saw that my husband was smiling, and he told me that the lawyer had called him and that the answer was finally yes and that we could stay."

Sonia Aguirre excuses herself for a moment and goes to her bedroom. When she returns to the couch she brings with her a large orange binder, carefully organized and full of her most precious possessions: the correspondence between her lawyer and the immigration and refugee board, their Permanent Resident Cards, and the letter of acceptance to Canada, complete with both an apology and an admission. Their file had been lost for a while, the official explained, and when it was eventually found and reviewed the government decided that the family could stay. At hearing the story once again, Fernando hugs his mom tightly. "When our parents got home and told us we could stay we had a big group hug! It was like a one-ton weight had lifted from my shoulders."

Sonia smiles at her son and kisses his cheek. "When we got the news, I saw something change in my children. I saw something new, something I hadn't seen before. They were happy, so happy. Finally, we all felt like we were truly part of this place, like we were safe. But it was still a little hard to believe until we went to the immigration office to pick up our Permanent Resident Cards. We met with the man we'd first seen in 2005 after we claimed refugee status. He was a big and serious-looking man with a large mustache, but he was so very kind and he smiled when he saw us. 'Welcome to Canada,' he said, and finally then I felt safe and secure. I feel like I'd lost three years of my life in the process—but it was worth it, it was all worth it."

When pressed, Sonia Aguirre admits that there are many things she still misses about Mexico. "I used to love the colourful festivals, the music, the food, the heat of the sun, and the beaches, of course." And she feels for her husband, a man forced into fleeing the country he loved. "It's difficult for him, with the language and the fact that he still can't work in his profession." But on the whole, Sonia knows in her heart she did the right thing for her children and wants people to know there is a dark side to her homeland—a side tourists in the all-inclusive resorts don't ever see.

"I think people and the government of Canada need to realize that Mexico is a very dangerous place," she says. "There's so much corruption and, when I see the news about the drugs and the violence and the killings, I feel bad for those who are still there. But we are safe. My goal in my life is to provide for my kids. I have done that and I am happy."

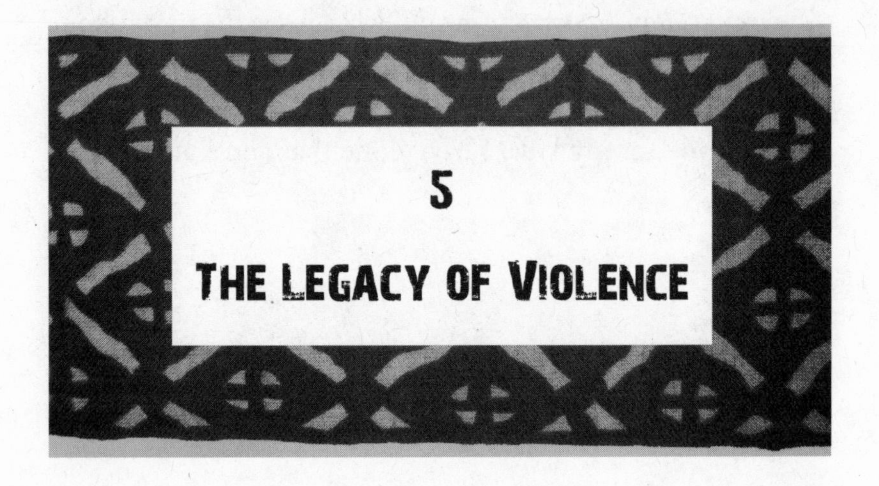

As a young boy in The Democratic Republic of Congo, Pierre* witnessed death on a massive scale. Then, in the exodus to a refugee camp outside the borders of his country, he suffered greatly. His family was torn apart by war, and his mother was forced to leave her husband behind in order to escape with Pierre and his siblings. The impact of these events left scars on the boy's heart far too deep to heal, and Pierre's time in Canada was not what his mother had hoped for. Pierre was constantly getting into fights, unable to regulate his emotions, oppositional to his teachers and school staff and, because of his limited language ability, chronically unsuccessful in his classes. Not surprisingly, Pierre found himself suspended multiple times. After being referred for outside counselling, he ended up in the district's alternate education programs. Ultimately, Pierre dropped out of school and onto the streets, where he became a very high-profile criminal.

Although Pierre was not so lucky, many of the students at Edmonds have been spared the trauma inflicted upon their parents and have suffered few, if any, ill effects from their exodus from the Middle East or Africa. But Pierre is not the only one to have witnessed—or even suffered directly from—acts of extreme violence aimed at their families or themselves. The legacy of such violence casts a dark shadow over many students as they attempt to settle into their new lives and, as it did with Pierre, often manifests itself as Post Traumatic Stress Disorder (PTSD). Despite our many success stories, Edmonds and Byrne Creek struggle to support too many students who have such complex emotional and mental health issues. The work is grinding, emotional and, at times, heartbreaking.

One of my own personal heartbreaks came in the form of a young boy named Willy,* whom I met during my first year at Byrne Creek. I'd never seen anyone quite like Willy before. The boy had come to Canada with his mother from Sierra Leone and had been in the country just a couple of months before Social Services intervened and removed him from his home. Parenting styles in other parts of the world often clash with societal and legal norms in North America, and what's considered a perfectly appropriate way to raise a child in one country is called abuse or neglect in another. On occasion, social workers move in to support refugee and immigrant families through the transition, but sometimes more than just support is required, and they are forced to move a child into foster care.

This was the case with Willy. The Ministry of Children and Family Development had found the boy a foster placement close to Byrne Creek, and his social worker had brought him in to register for Grade 8. While Luc and many of the other African students were quiet, Willy was a little pinball—a short boy with large round cheeks, a mop of curly hair, sparking eyes, and a wonderful smile. He bounced around the school at will, a bundle of energy who soon became a familiar sight in the hallways. Like many of the other West Africans in the school, Willy could hardly read a word, but his spoken English was fine, although when animated, his lyrical Krio accent and staccato style of talking frequently made him almost impossible to understand.

Willy was irrepressible, taking everything—his removal from his home, his foster placement, his frequent trips to my office—in stride. He was always smiling, always happy to see Vice Principal Ron Hall or me whenever he was shipped down to us so we could deal with one incident after another—none of which, he claimed, were ever his fault. To put it mildly, Willy had challenges managing his interpersonal relationships.

There were a handful of other African boys in his grade, from Sudan and Rwanda in particular, with whom he had encounters. Once he even sent himself down to see me after getting into a fight with a Sudanese boy. I asked him what happened. "He made me sad," he replied in his musical voice, his big eyes brimming with tears. "He made fun of how I talked English and so I hit him." The irony of the encounter was that Willy's combatant could hardly string two sentences together himself.

Willy also liked to collect interesting things. He had an MP3 player that didn't work, a bike without functioning brakes that was two sizes too small for him and, one day, a very expensive-looking camera. It was hard not to think he'd stolen it, but Willy adamantly claimed he'd found it outside the Value Village thrift store on Edmonds Street. The camera had been confiscated by a teacher and brought to the office. A name and a phone number were written on a piece of tape on the back, so I called the number, bracing myself for the news that the camera had indeed been stolen. I didn't want to think that Willy was a thief, but experience with other students had made me reluctant to believe fanciful stories.

A woman answered the phone. I introduced myself and told her why I was calling. She asked for a description of the camera and when I provided it, she drew a deep breath and told me that the camera had been part of a large number of items she'd cleaned out of her house in Vancouver's exclusive Shaughnessy neighbourhood and donated to charity several months earlier. She had no idea how the thing had made its way to Edmonds, but she was certain it hadn't been stolen and, as far as she was concerned, it legitimately belonged to Willy now. Relieved, I gave it back to the boy who triumphantly deposited it in his backpack.

We put a lot of work into Willy. Despite the headaches he caused, he was genuinely a likeable little boy, and headway was being made at school, when something happened at his foster home. Willy was not the sort of boy who followed rules easily and, after a while, his foster parents gave up on him and returned him to his social worker. This was problematic for Willy and for us, since the only place they could find for him to stay, at least for the short term, was a group home some fifteen kilometres away.

Willy had no way of getting to Byrne Creek every day, and since the group home setting was supposed to be a temporary placement, no transportation would be provided. But it made no sense to enrol Willy in the neighbourhood school either, since it was in a completely different school district and most likely unaccustomed to boys like him. There was, however, one option: the group home was not very far from my house and, to keep Willy at Byrne Creek, we decided that he would commute with me.

And so, for the next couple of weeks, we travelled together. When I pulled into the driveway in front of the group home to pick him up, Willy was always ready. He would have his backpack on and be standing outside, waiting for me. On the drive to school, we talked about whatever subject came up: his classes, the other kids in the home, or his hopes for the future. Occasionally he brought up his mother. He was never angry or upset about how things had worked out, but he maintained a level of hope that maybe one day he'd be able to go home again. In the meantime, however, he had more pressing things on his mind. Like a belt.

Willy had very few clothes and what he did have was ragged, the wrong size, or hopelessly out of fashion. His shoes were held together by little more than a few fragments of leather and his pants sagged so much he spent half the day pulling them up. Willy had never owned his own belt, he confided, and wanted to know if I had one at home I could give him. I told that story to my wife Sharon, and she insisted we could do better than give him a second-hand belt. And so, the following weekend, Sharon, Willy, I, and our son Aidan, not yet one at the time, went on a shopping trip to the neighbourhood Walmart.

Sharon had as much fun as Willy, cruising the aisles, picking out jeans, shirts, shoes, and, of course, his very own belt. Willy got on very well with my wife, and he was also very good with my son, talking to him and making him laugh. Willy asked me what I thought about a particular pair of pants and, since I'm not particularly well known for my fashion sense, I deferred to my wife. "Ask the boss," I told him. Willy looked at me in shock.

"But you are the boss!" he protested. "You're a vice principal."

"Maybe at work," I replied, "but we're not at work now."

A couple of hundred dollars later, we were done. We drove Willy back to his home and, as he got out, loaded down with bags, he thanked us gratefully. "See you later, boss," he said to Sharon before he shut the door.

It became our little joke over the time we commuted together. "Say hello to the boss," Willy would say as I dropped him off at the group home each day.

"I will," I promised, and sure enough as soon as I got home I dutifully conveyed the message.

Within a couple of weeks, Willy was placed with another family in Burnaby, but one still a great distance from Byrne Creek. Although they reluctantly agreed to bring him to us, Willy still struggled, and there were many times we had to call his foster parents to come and pick him up for one infraction or another. With both the frequency of the trouble and the time it took to get him from the school, we finally came to the realization that it would be in everyone's best interests if Willy enrolled at his new neighbourhood school and got a fresh start. On his last day, we said goodbye, shook hands and, not without a touch of sadness, I watched him go. The Willy experiment at Byrne Creek had certainly been interesting.

I wondered how Willy was doing from time to time, but as the months passed and other students enrolled and other issues emerged, he faded from my mind. I left Byrne, moved onto Edmonds, and had almost forgotten him when our paths crossed once again. I was taking some students on a field trip when a young man approached me on the street and said hello. I had no idea who he was until he stuck out his hand and in a voice I instantly recognized said, "Hello, Mr. Stah." The bus was waiting to take the children back to school, and we had no time to talk, so I told Willy where I was working and invited him to come by for a visit.

Two weeks later he showed up. The short, round-faced boy I'd driven to school was gone, replaced by a tall, thin young man, now nearly nineteen years old. Life had not been as kind to him as he would have liked, Willy explained. The foster placement that had taken him out of Byrne had not lasted, nor had several other placements after it. He'd never gone back home and currently he was living in another group home. He'd bounced from school to school as well, he explained, things not working out for him at any of them.

Still, Willy was optimistic that everything would turn out for the best. His social worker was going to help him get back to school, he explained, and he still held out hope that one day he would go home to live with his mother. We sat and talked for a while, catching up. He asked after my son and was thrilled to hear Aidan was ready to start kindergarten. "I like him. He's a good boy," Willy said. "Smart too."

"And how is Mrs. Stah?" he asked as he was leaving my office.

"She's doing very well," I replied.

"Good. I like her too," he said. Before shutting the door, he paused and turned back to me. "Goodbye Mr. Stah, and don't forget to say hello to the boss for me."

I thanked him for the visit and wished him good luck, truly meaning it. Willy had suffered great trauma in Sierra Leone and, since his arrival in Canada, life had been cruel to him. Nonetheless, Willy still found reasons to hope and to believe that good things would happen. A big part of me hoped that things would change for Willy too, and for all the traumatized children who came after him—because they most certainly will keep coming.

Events around the globe have instant and dramatic ramifications in the hallways of Edmonds Community School. Today's headlines are forewarnings of the next wave of refugee children coming to the school tomorrow. The disintegration of Yugoslavia brought a flood of Croat and Kosovar students to Burnaby; the chaos in Afghanistan brought Afghan students; and if a war erupts in Sudan or Sierra Leone, twelve months later a rush of Africans will arrive at our doors.

By the same token, a massacre in a refugee camp, a car bomb in Baghdad, or a rocket attack on Kabul doesn't kill strangers from across the world, it kills the friends and family of Edmonds students—and, in an instant, it can bring back the trauma that often lies just under the surface. Rape, malnutrition, injuries caused by bombs, machetes, bullets, and psychological torment are not things simply left behind at the airport. Chris Friesen, Director of Settlement Services for Immigrant Services Society, knows all too well that many families coming into Canada from refugee backgrounds have suffered grievous physical and emotional wounds and that many refugees require counselling. Though it is far less than what is needed, in 2009 ISS began providing refugees with mental health support from a psychologist. "For the children from refugee camps especially," Friesen says, "the earlier the intervention, the better."

For those of us at Edmonds and at Byrne Creek, the critical question is how we can best support such intervention. According to Elin Horton, along with giving them lots of love, one significant way to get through to traumatized children is through art. "Like nothing else," she argued, "art opens up the lines of communication with English language learners, especially traumatized ones. To see a picture of burning houses and tanks firing, to see pictures of men with guns and broken bodies lying on the ground, and then to look at the artist and realize it's a six-year-old boy who's drawn that picture? To see the world through his eyes? To experience his personal history? That's powerful."

Still, it often it takes more than just art to help the most fragile of students, and Edmonds has much more support than a typical elementary school. There is no magic bullet that will solve the problems that refugee and immigrant students must face at school, but teachers, senior district administrators, and elected trustees do know what helps. It boils down to six things: small class sizes; adequate levels of ESL and learning-assistance support; enough educational assistants to provide one-on-one support to the most vulnerable students; counselling services in the school to work with students with emotional and behavioural challenges; money to provide food, school supplies, clothes, and opportunities; and, finally, having the right staff in the right placements.

The first five of these factors require money far in excess of what is required to service an equivalent number of students at a middle-class school—and school board trustees and senior administrators need both foresight and courage to commit the required dollars. It's expensive no doubt, but as Lorraine Hodgson, head counsellor at Byrne Creek, frequently says, it's "pay me now or pay me later, baby." And she is absolutely right. Societies that aren't willing to put the appropriate level of resources into early literacy and early intervention will pay an exponentially higher price in later years as disaffected students drop out and put an incredible strain on the welfare, criminal justice, and healthcare systems.

The sixth critical piece is having the right people in place. It isn't just about the number of teachers in a school, but who they are: their skill set and their attitudes. At Edmonds, the people who work as counsellors and behavioural support staff epitomize the necessary level of exceptional service. Nora Mora (counselling), Michelle LePoole (counselling), and Nancy Robson (youth and childcare) primarily help students deal with the day-to-day issues that arise. Jaynie Miller (ESL teacher) runs art-therapy sessions and Ginny Tahara (a counsellor with almost three decades at Edmonds) focuses more on the family as a unit.

Adequate behavioural support is absolutely critical for Edmonds neighbourhood students because many of them have not had opportunities to practise behaving appropriately or regulating their own behaviour. Upwards of fifty times a day, students go to Room 106, the Problem Solving Room. That the majority of the referrals are students making the choice themselves to seek help with a problem speaks to the success of Robson, Mora, and LePoole—who use the room as their home base.

The focus in Room 106 is on managing one's self, on teaching explicit social situation skills, and on learning to deal with rejection, disappointment, and problems with peers. There is also an element of proactive management, something Michelle LePoole is particularly good at. Knowing certain students have challenges with particular activities, transitions, and changes—such as working with a substitute teacher—Michelle will gather these students up and work with them in her room to prevent problems before they occur.

Thanks to Ginny Tahara, the circle of care extends far beyond the classroom. Ginny's own history, as the daughter of Japanese Canadians who were interned in 1942 and then resettled after the end of the Second World War, allows her a bond of understanding with refugee families. Armed with diverse teaching experience and holding a master's degree in counselling psychology, Ginny has been helping children and parents at Edmonds since 1981.

Much has changed in those thirty years. "Take Hillside Gardens, for instance," Ginny says. "The complex used to be called Sylvan Gardens or something like that—and it wasn't a nice place—there were lots of drugs and violence. But by the mid 1980s, the Vietnamese and some Central Americans—Salvadorans, I think, or maybe Nicaraguans fleeing from war—moved in, and both the complex and the neighbourhood started to change. Then people from the Balkans, Afghans, Africans, and Iraqis came, and now Hillside is a mini United Nations."

Elin Horton's theme of hope resonates with Ginny as well. "Refugees are so hopeful about Canada and the future here for their children," she says, "but they are also people who have suffered and have seen such violence. It can be very sad listening to their stories, and it takes work to see that hope realized. Some families are very educated, some are not, but no matter what their background, we educate their children and facilitate their transition into our country and culture and help it become their country and culture, too."

Ginny's ability to listen and to facilitate that transition is her gift to the families of the Edmonds neighbourhood. She continues to work with both parents and children, runs women's groups for immigrant and refugee mothers and, in partnership with retired Burnaby counsellor Helen Stolte, administers the Burnaby Children's Fund, a local charity that provides thousands of dollars in clothes, food, bus passes, and other material support for disadvantaged students and their families.

After almost thirty years at Edmonds, Ginny has experienced it all—the hope and despair, the wins and losses, the successes and failures—and she has rejoiced, raged, and wept with countless students and their families. Through it all, she had been profoundly moved by the strength and resilience she has been privileged to witness.

6
THREE SIMPLE WISHES

Ten-year-old Mehari Tesfamariam had an uncanny skill for knowing when important visitors were in the building. Without fail, whenever a Member of Parliament, city councillor, police officer, or visiting board-level administrator arrived at Edmonds, Mehari's skinny frame and unruly shock of hair would bounce down the hallway.

Today was no different. "Who are you?" he asked politely, without any sense of intimidation, at the sight of the visiting VIP I was touring through the building.

"I'm Mr. Kardaal, the Assistant Superintendant of the School District," the guest announced.

"Oh," Mehari said with obvious disappointment, as I

Mehari Tesfamariam

struggled to keep from laughing. "I thought you were Mr. Starr's older brother—and fatter brother, too," the boy hissed to me conspiratorially in what I'm sure he thought was a whisper but must have been loud enough for anyone in the hallway, including my smiling boss, to hear.

Kardaal was not the first senior school district

administrator to meet Mehari, but his skills at hosting dignitaries reached their apogee on the day the superintendant, Claudio Morelli, arrived for his annual visit. Morelli had been in the school less than thirty seconds when Mehari strode confidently up to us. "Who's this guy?" he asked me, studying our visitor intently.

"Who do you think I am?" an amused Morelli replied.

"I dunno, a magician maybe?" Mehari answered. "In that black suit you look like a magician."

"Mehari, this is Mr. Morelli, the most important man in the school district," I interrupted.

At that the boy's eyes lit up as a huge smile creased his face. "Holy cow," Mehari exclaimed, very much impressed. "You must be the guy in charge of hot lunch!"

When I sit down to talk with Mehari's father, Andebrihan (Andy) Tesfamariam, a devoted father of six, I can immediately see where the boy gets his enthusiasm. For Andy, that enthusiasm is directed, in part, to his modest aspirations for the future. "I would like to be a custodian. That is my hope," he says. "I would be happy with that, to clean a place, to make it look good, and to earn a decent wage so that I can look after my family and allow them to continue their education at college." A job, a family, and an education for his children—three simple wishes for things that are generally taken for granted in the West. But when Andy and his wife, Wubet Elquebit, see their school-age children—Mehari, Helen, and Zemen—playing and happily attending classes at Edmonds, they understand how precious those wishes are and they do not regret the immense price they have paid just to have the chance to achieve them.

Andy grew up in a thatch-roofed stone home in a place

called Andaqworqs, a small farming village in Eritrea, a province of Ethiopia. Nestled in the shadow of the mountains, it was far from the bustle of the provincial capital of Asmara and farther still from the metropolis of Addis Ababa. The fourth of Tesfamariam Gebr and Yehdaga Gebrmical's six children, Andy attended the Ethiopian Orthodox Church school when he turned five and tended to his father's goats on the stony plains outside the village when his lessons ended.

At eight years of age, Andy transferred to the public school. It was there that he became aware of the troubled relationship between Eritrea and the rest of Ethiopia. Andy clearly remembers politics being openly discussed in his elementary school. "Mostly I had good experiences at school," he says. "I liked to read and write and I was happy as a child, but we knew there were problems and we were always worrying about the government in Addis Ababa. Soldiers would arrive from time to time at our village, and we all believed that they didn't like the Tigrinya people and wanted us off our land."

There was good reason to think such things in the late 1970s. Eritrea—with its strategic location, coastline, and natural resources—was a vital, if reluctant, province of Ethiopia. The connection began in 1952 when the one-time British colony was awarded to Ethiopia in a UN-mandated federation. Eritrea was to maintain a significant degree of autonomy, but within a short time, Addis Ababa decreed Amharic, the language of the south, to be the language of instruction in all Eritrean schools. This mandate was the latest in a series of moves deemed unacceptable by the Tigrinya-speaking majority in Eritrea and provided yet another reason for the newly formed Eritrean Liberation Front to take up arms against the Ethiopian government. Thus began a forty-year struggle for independence.

In 1984—the same year that famine was making international headlines for Bob Geldof and his Band Aid relief efforts—another much smaller, though no less pivotal, event for Andy Tesfamariam occurred in Ethiopia: "In 1984 Ethiopian officials came to my town and said I had to go and do my military service in the army. This was not a comfortable position for me—but what choice did I have? So they took me from my family and sent me to a place called Harr, a town near the Somali border. There was a military camp there and this was where I did my army training."

But Tesfamariam and the other reluctant Eritrean recruits were taught more than just combat skills. "At Harr they tried to educate—re-educate I suppose—us Eritreans in politics," Tesfamariam explains. "They tried to teach us that the Ethiopian government was good for us and that they really loved the Eritrean people and only hated the guerrillas who were fighting for our independence. They told us the guerrillas were the bad guys and then they trained us to kill them by teaching us how to fight and how to use rifles, machine guns, and grenades."

After six months at Harr, Andy's training was complete and in 1985 he was sent back to Eritrea with his military unit. "We engaged in war and many people died," he explains. "The Ethiopian artillery would shell a village and then, because I spoke Tigrinya, I'd be ordered to go into what was left of the place with food and tell the people to come out of hiding. I would tell them that their government loved them and that we were here to protect them from the guerrillas."

For the next five years, Andy's life would be one of shelling villages and fighting. Then, in 1990, he was almost killed during a particularly vicious fire fight with Eritrean rebels. He lifts up his shirt to show a large, circular bullet scar above his heart. "This should have killed me," he says, turning slightly sideways to reveal a massive indent in his rib cage. "A machine gun ripped a large part of my chest away, and I don't know how I lived." Gravely injured and not sure he would live to see his twenty-fifth birthday, Andy was shipped to a military hospital where he spent a full year convalescing from his wounds. In 1991 he was deemed unfit for military service and was discharged from the army and allowed to go home to his village. He was given a pension of eighty-five Ethiopian birr (about eight US dollars) per month.

In May 1991, just after Andy's discharge from the army, Addis Ababa fell to the advancing rebels. By this time, Eritrea was, for all intents and purposes, free of Ethiopian control, and the mood in the country was optimistic, even though a bitter war was on the horizon. Andy Tesfamariam had made the transition back to civilian life: he had married (a relationship which ended in divorce), had two sons, who are now adults and still living in Eritrea, and, when the fighting stopped, he was in Asmara wholesaling coffee and an ancient African grain called teff.

Andy describes how, soon after his divorce, he met his current wife Wubet and they quickly fell in love with each other. Wubet, however, has a different version of the story. "Not so fast, Andy," she laughs. "That's not how it was. Don't forget about your girlfriends! He had a lot of girlfriends," she laughs. "Too many!" Tesfamariam smiles meekly and ruefully admits that Wubet is right. As for her falling quickly in love with him? Wubet has a far different recollection of that event as well.

"What really happened was that we met in 1998. We came from neighbouring villages, and Andy was an acquaintance of my mother. He liked me and suggested to her that he marry me, but I was not feeling like this was a very good idea. I was only seventeen and he was a thirty-two-year-old man. Plus, he was divorced with two sons. And don't forget—he had lots of girlfriends!" But, under pressure from her mother, Wubet eventually relented. "She said to me 'Come on, he's a good guy, he's good looking, he's a businessman, and he even has a pension from the army! What's wrong with him?' I suppose that I listened and eventually I married him."

The couple moved back to his village, and Wubet was soon pregnant with her first son, Mehari. Andy was working and life was good when, in 1998, Ethiopia and Eritrea became embroiled in a short but particularly brutal war and, once again, Andy found himself reluctantly involved in combat. "This time," he explains, "Eritrean officials came to our house and said I had to go and fight. I said I was wounded and I asked not to go and they told me it didn't matter. 'Yes, I'd been hurt, yes I'd been considered unfit for the Ethiopian army,' they said, but that was the *Ethiopian* army, they explained, and I would do just fine for the Eritrean army. Then they gave me a gun, said that I was now the security for the village, and that I was to keep my eyes open for Ethiopians."

About to give birth, Wubet did not take the news well. "My husband was unfit and I didn't want him to go. He'd already been hurt in war, and I was angry there was another war, very angry at Eritrea for making him do it. And," she adds looking sideways at her husband, "a little mad at him for going, too."

Andy's initial role in the war was limited to patrolling his village until, ten months or so after the birth of Mehari, he was called in and told that with the fighting between Ethiopia and Eritrea becoming increasingly bitter and, with the independence of his country in jeopardy, it was time for him to step up and return to full combat. "This was a very difficult time for us all," Andy explains. "I was off fighting somewhere; half of Eritrea was controlled by us and the other half by the Ethiopians. Then I got news that the fighting was close to the village, and I was very worried about my family."

Andy had every reason to worry. He'd learned that Wubet and Mehari, along with the other residents, had fled their homes and were hiding from the advancing Ethiopians in the mountains outside their village. Desperate to find his wife and child, Andy left his unit and went to an aunt's house nearby to ask if she had recent word about the situation back home. She confirmed his worst fears and, after feeding and sheltering him, gave Andy civilian clothes so that he could leave the army to go find his family.

Andy spent two fruitless days looking and then went to the house of another relative, an uncle this time, and asked if he had news. His uncle repeated the story that the villagers were hiding somewhere in the hills, but with the Ethiopian army active in the area, there was no way for Andy to look for them. Then, at the worst possible moment, Andy was captured by the Ethiopian army. Dressed in civilian clothes or not, they quickly discovered he was a soldier and he was sent south to a military prisoner-of-war camp in Ethiopia—a place where he would spend the better part of the next two years, helpless to send or receive word about the fate of his wife and child.

"Wubet and Mehari eventually returned to our village, but they had no idea if I was alive or dead and I didn't know if they were safe either," he says, "until one day in 2002 when an official came to the camp and gave us three choices. We could go back to Eritrea, stay in Ethiopia, or take our chances at a nearby refugee camp in Waila Nihby."

The fighting had stopped, and the two countries were negotiating their border with help from the UN, but Ethiopia was an openly hostile place for Eritreans and, not wanting to return to the chaos of his homeland, Andy opted for the safety of the refugee camp. Once there, he quickly sent word to his village that he was safe. Remarkably, Wubet and his son had survived the war as well and, by October 2002, the family was reunited.

The family grew by one the following year with the addition of their new baby daughter, Helen, who was born in the camp. Despite the safety it afforded, the Tesfamariam family quickly appreciated just how difficult life in a refugee camp could be. "It was a hard place," Wubet remembers. "We were given fifteen kilograms of food per month and we would wait in line for everything. Wait in line for food, wait for water, wait for cooking oil. It was so bad, and so dangerous, too. We lived in grass huts and many times cooking fires would cause sparks to fly that set the houses on fire. This woman who lived near us—she had no children or husband—one night her house caught on fire. It burned so quickly, she had nobody to help her get out and she died."

The Tesfamariam Family: Andy, Abraham, Wubet, and Madeline

Andy's family did not escape tragedy during the conflict. After his release from prison, he learned his father had died of illness and two brothers and two sisters had perished in the conflict as well. There was no reason to return to Eritrea now, and a new life far from their war-ravaged country seemed to be an increasingly attractive proposition.

"We could apply to Canada, New Zealand, or Australia," Andy says, "and I thought I knew something about Canada. Before the war, I was in the port city of Massawa on the Red Sea and I saw these boats unloading truck after truck of bags of grain that said 'Gift from Canada' or something like that and I thought 'Wow! Oh my goodness! This must be a rich country to give away so much food!'"

By 2005 the United Nations High Commissioner for Refugees approved his claim and, with permission to go to Canada established, the Tesfamariam family flew to Vancouver where they were greeted at the airport and sent to Welcome House. Andy remembers tearing up with happiness when they got there, but Wubet had a very different reaction. "I hated Welcome House! I was very pregnant with our daughter Zemen and so I was stuck upstairs in bed in our apartment while Andy was doing the banking and the paperwork. Then, for some reason, I started to panic. I'd hardly seen him for two days and I thought that maybe he'd left me in this place and had gone back to Eritrea!"

Although exceedingly grateful to be safe in Canada, both Wubet and Andy remember their first year as being very difficult. Andy took English classes while Wubet looked after three children. Then, with what he thought was a proficient command of the language, Andy was hired at a glass company. But he was let go after three months. "My English just wasn't good enough," he explains. "Then I took coursework to become a security guard but I failed it once again because of my English. I got a job in Calgary and went there to work while Wubet and the kids stayed here, but the company went bankrupt, owing me several thousand dollars of salary."

With that money still outstanding, Andy returned to Vancouver and, as the years passed, his family continued to grow with the addition of Zahra, Abraham, and Madeline. "Six kids is a lot, I know," he says. "It's difficult to explain, but in Africa we're raised with the notion that having many children is a good thing because they'll look after you, but it is very difficult in Canada. I was talking to this man from Sudan one day over coffee, and he said he was really struggling because he had six kids and was trying to provide for them. I said I completely understand!"

Then as now, Andy and Wubet live for their children, three of whom currently attend school at Edmonds. Zemen is in Grade 1 while Helen is in Grade 2. Although the girls are a year apart, they could be twins with their pretty faces and long, thick, curly hair. Sharp-witted, smart, and playful, the two are a whirlwind of activity—just like their big brother Mehari, who is in Grade 6. Kind, hard-working, and sensitive, eleven-year-old Mehari is a fixture in the school, getting there early to play basketball in the gym and volunteering as a lunch monitor.

Even with her three other children—Madeline, Abraham, and Zahra—too young to attend classes, Wubet still finds time to give back to the school and the community. Looking for a way to belong and something meaningful to do, she found both a job serving students breakfast and a friend in Doreen George, Edmonds' Community Coordinator, and has become an integral part of the school community. She brings the little ones with her, and they putter around the cafeteria or visit friends in Strong Start, the parent-participation preschool in the room next to the cafeteria.

Although they have been in Canada for six years now, Andy and Wubet have dreams yet to be fulfilled and chapters yet to be written. "I dream of going back to Eritrea so that my husband can visit his mother and his sister," Wubet explains, "to see them one last time. But we can't afford it just now."

Still, they are happy. After all, it was for their children that they came here in the first place. "I want my children to be successful," Wubet says, "I want them to have a good future." And, as much as he thinks of his past, it is the future that Andy focuses on these days. "We very recently took on Canadian citizenship," he says proudly. "I am so proud of that. I now belong to this country and I will contribute."

7

THIS IS WHAT WAR LOOKS LIKE TO WOMEN

"There's someone here to see you," said my secretary, Karen Dawson, "and it's important, by the looks of things." I got up from my desk and went out into the main office to see a large set of big brown eyes looking up at me from beside the counter. It was Sandra* Freeman's daughter, all of seven years old, hair tied back in a bow and looking very serious, a small workbook in her hand.

"I want to read you something," she said. Students regularly came to the office to read to me or our vice principal. We encouraged it and really looked forward to the visits.

"What do you want to read?" I asked sitting down in a chair and motioning for her to do the same.

"My book about me," she declared proudly, clambering

up into the chair and opening her workbook up to the first page. "I wrote it all by myself and I did the pictures, too," she explained, pointing at a drawing of herself. And then the girl took a deep breath. "My name is…" she said, launching into her story. She read slowly and deliberately, stumbling on the occasional word. But, with minimal help and growing confidence, she read her entire story, explained her pictures and, when she was done, thanked me for listening, proudly shut the book, excused herself from the office, and skipped happily back to class.

"She's come a long way," Karen said from behind her desk, and she was right. The child *had* progressed—although, as impressive as her emerging reading skills were, considering the ordeal her mother went through to bring her to safety, the true miracle was not that the girl could read a simple story, but that she was alive at all.

After decades of relative peace, civil war broke out in the small west African nation of Liberia in 1980. After a series of repressive regimes and upheavals, the country again degenerated into civil war in 1990. Over the next fifteen years, approximately a quarter of a million Liberians were killed in the violence. Many others fled and settled in neighbouring Ivory Coast, a country once safe for refugees, until civil war broke out there as well and Liberian fighters become actively involved in the fighting on the side of the rebels. When this happened, all Liberians were quickly targeted by the Ivory Coast military. One of those people was nineteen-year-old Sandra Freeman.

Sandra was born in 1982 in a small village far from the capital city of Monrovia, well past the place where the paved road ends. "My town," she remembers, "was a place of mud houses with thatch and zinc roofs deep in the forest, the sort of place one comes from but seldom goes to. I was the youngest of nine children and when I was just a little girl, my mother, who wanted our lives to have promise, sent us to Monrovia, the capital, to live with my uncle. She didn't have the means to send us to school herself, you see, but my uncle had a government job and wanted to help his poor relations and so we went to the city to be educated."

In 1989 when she was just seven, the war that would rip both Liberia and her family apart began. "I would hear about it from my cousins who would say fearfully, 'the rebels are coming!'" she explains. "I was just a little girl and I didn't understand what that meant. I thought rebels were robots and they weren't human like me. But then I saw them and learned that they were people—although I'd soon find out that they could do the most inhuman of things."

Sandra's opportunity to go to school evaporated when the war forced the government to shut down the schools. Though she was very young, Sandra's memories of the day the rebels first came to her house are etched permanently in her mind. "We hid in the house when the first group came. We heard them outside, heard the shooting and the screaming and the shouting, and one came right up to our house and yelled inside. 'Who's there? Come out!' he said, but we didn't and instead lay hidden under our beds, beside the concrete walls. My uncle's house was by the beach, and we'd filled sandbags and stacked them by the windows to stop the bullets from penetrating the house, but still we lay on the floor beside those thick walls and prayed they would keep us safe."

Desperate to find sanctuary, her uncle put the children

in his car and drove across town to the US embassy, hoping the Americans would let them in because of his position in the government. It is at this point in her story that the tears first well up in Sandra's eyes. "I saw such terrible things as we travelled to the embassy. The streets were in chaos. Dead bodies lay on the ground, soldiers with guns standing over them. The road was lined with burning houses and cars and little children—some just babies, either killed or alone, crying for their dead parents.

"Of all the things I saw that day, I remember most this lady who'd left her children alone at her house to try to find them food, but because of the fighting she couldn't get back home, and so she just stood there on the street screaming and crying, putting her head in her hands and shouting, 'My children! My children!' But she couldn't do anything to help those babies. No one could. I don't know what happened to her and her children. This is what war looks like to women."

Sandra's hopes for refuge were dashed by the locked gates of the American Embassy. "They wouldn't let us enter and so we huddled outside the gates as the bullets flew and we hoped that being close to the Americans would protect us. After a while, the fighting ceased and so we left and went back home."

The civil war in Liberia was not one of constant battles; instead, the fighting ebbed and flowed as rebel groups gained strength and lost it. Life would be peaceful for a time and it would seem as if normalcy had returned to the country, then it would be shattered by the next rebel offensive. Through it all, Sandra and her family survived, praying for peace and hiding by the thick concrete walls when the rebel forces swept through their neighbourhood.

"I continued to grow up, but I didn't have any schooling," she says. "There was no childhood for me, just hiding and running and waiting for peace that never came. Finally, things got so bad again that the war scattered our family to the wind and, when I was fifteen, me and my sister Julia ended up in Ivory Coast."

For a while, life in Ivory Coast was good. In 2001 Sandra even met a man named John, a fellow Liberian, and the two fell in love. Only nineteen, Sandra was soon pregnant and was planning to build a life and a family with the man she loved. Though her country was still engulfed in violence, the two had plans to return and seek out their families as soon as peace arrived. But things would not work out the way they planned. War soon came to Ivory Coast itself, and the hiding and the dying started all over again.

As she talks about the second round of fighting, the tears that she stubbornly kept from falling begin to tumble from Sandra's eyes once more. I tell her she doesn't have to continue the interview if she doesn't want to, but Sandra shakes her head vigorously and pushes ahead, determined to tell a story never told to an outsider before. "No," she says. "You need to hear—the world needs to hear what happened. The Ivorians wanted us Liberians gone, you see. Many Liberian rebels were fighting now in Ivory Coast and the army decided to kill us, to hunt us all down, rebels or not. We found that out on the day we went shopping to the market. We were on the street when we heard a noise, a sound like an earthquake, and I didn't know what it was when suddenly everyone was running, running away from something. And then I saw the helicopter. It was an Ivory Coast military gunship and it was heading toward the crowd—toward me.

"I was clumsy, I guess from being pregnant, and when I started to run from the helicopter I fell down. When I got up and started to run again, the guns of the helicopter fired and the smell of smoke and gunpowder and blood filled the air. The shrieks of people were all around me and I looked for my sister but she wasn't there. She was gone. You understand what I mean by that? My man was God knows where too, dead for all I knew, and I had no one left to help me and so I followed a group of Liberians into the bush.

"The jungle was such a scary place. You'd hear the soldiers talking, looking for you, their voices echoing through the trees, and you had to be quiet, so quiet. We were so thirsty as well, but there was no clean water in the jungle, just these holes in the ground full of dirty water. But we drank it anyway, because that's what you do when you're thirsty and you have no choice. But the worst were the snakes. There were so many. I'm scared of snakes, you know, and I remembered the saying we have in Liberia that if you see a snake, don't embarrass it and it won't bother you. I tried real hard not to embarrass those snakes, and stayed out of their way as they coiled in the branches or slithered through the bush around me."

The small group of Liberians wanted nothing more than to just get to safety, and with the peaceful country of Ghana just to the east and with a large population of Liberians already living there in refugee camps, they started walking toward the border. "We just walked and walked until we came to a checkpoint where some Ivory Coast rebels were," Sandra explains.

"The rebels in Liberia and Ivory Coast were all the same. Young men, some even boys, and when you saw them, you always had to pretend that you supported them, that you liked them, and you learned to smile and approve of the things they said and the things they did—because if you didn't, they would kill you. I thought I knew how to talk to rebels, but we still didn't want to have to deal with them and so we tried to sneak around the checkpoint. But they saw us and so we had no choice but to come out of the bush and onto the road and take our chances with these men. At the checkpoint, these twelve or so gunmen said to us, 'Here is our enemy!' But we said, 'No, we're just some Liberians trying to find a safe place to be. Please let us go through.' But they didn't let us pass. And then it happened. I don't like to talk about it, don't like even thinking about what happened to me that day. It was so unfair. But life isn't fair, you know?

"These three rebels came to me, smiling. They pointed their guns at me and said, 'Let's go.' I said, 'Why? Why do you want me to go with you? And where?' I said I was tired and that I didn't want to go anywhere, but they ignored my protests, didn't care that I just wanted to rest. They took me away from the group and then they pushed me to the ground real rough, and then they went on me. I was pregnant and so I pleaded for them to let me go. I begged these men to stop. I said, 'Please don't hurt me,' but they told me they'd either do this thing or they'd kill me. And so they took their turns on me—all three of them, raping me. They were like animals and it hurt so much, so very much."

Shaken, bleeding, and violated, Sandra was released to join the rest of the Liberians. As they continued their journey east, the group soon came upon a small town near the Ghanaian frontier where they were welcomed and fed, but after her horrific ordeal, Sandra had little appetite. "I just wished that I would die and I didn't much feel like food. But we were now very close to the Ghanaian border and this made me happy because I knew Ghana was a peaceful place and we would be safe."

They crossed the border without incident, and soon after arriving in Ghana came across Médecins Sans Frontières. Sandra told the doctors what had happened to her, and they quickly started her on a cocktail of pills and injections to prevent HIV. "I was very scared because they confirmed I was several months pregnant, and I was worried that maybe what those men did to me or maybe the drugs I had to take would affect my baby."

Sandra and the others were sent to a refugee camp, and she quickly set about looking for John, but he was nowhere in the camp and so she went to the United Nations High Commissioner for Refugees and asked them to help her look for him. Remarkably, John was found alive. But the news was bittersweet: he was nowhere close—nowhere in Ghana, for that matter. He was on the other side of the Ivory Coast in a refugee camp in Guinea. Sandra wrote a letter to him and let him know she was safe. When the fighting died down and it was safer to travel, she travelled to Guinea to see John and tell him that he would be a father. And there was something else Sandra needed to confess to her man as well.

"I told him what happened to me, what those men in the Ivory Coast did to me," she says. "I was scared to tell him that, and ashamed, but he's a good man and he was so happy to see me again and he told me he loved me no matter what. And then we got married." John had news as well. With no idea what had happened to Sandra and doubting very much she was still alive after the carnage in the marketplace, he had successfully applied for resettlement and would soon be travelling to a new home in Canada.

"Of course I was so happy for him," says Sandra, "but I was also worried for me and our child and I feared we'd be stuck in the camp. But John promised that, as soon as he could, he'd bring me and the baby over to Canada. He told me we were his life and he'd make sure we were safe. He promised me this and then we said goodbye and he left for Canada and I returned to the camp in Ghana."

Sandra does not like speaking about her experiences in the refugee camp and that is something Chris Friesen, the Director of Settlement Services for ISS, completely understands. Friesen is eminently qualified to speak on the subject of refugee camps and the experiences of those who endure them. He began his career working with the refugee community twenty-five years ago as a coordinator and educational counsellor for the Windle Charitable Trust.

Based in Lokichogio, Kenya, near the Kakuma refugee camp, Friesen worked with Sudanese refugees at approximately the same time that Amel Madut and Nyiwer Chol arrived in that region. Today, Friesen leads the team of first-language support workers, volunteers, and counsellors charged with supporting recently arrived refugees in their first critical days, weeks, and months. No matter what country a refugee may be from—Afghanistan, Democratic Republic of the Congo, Sudan, or Liberia—Friesen explains, surviving both the journey to a refugee camp and the camp itself can be very traumatizing. When asked how families manage in that first few weeks after arrival, Friesen pauses, knowing the complexity of the question.

"The reality differs for each person based on the size of their family and the situation they come from," he says. "Their own makeup, trauma, the conditions of the refugee camp are all factors, and so is the time they've had to ready themselves for the journey. Some people have weeks if not months to prepare for their trip to Canada, while others in high-risk situations are often put in hiding and frequently have forty-eight hours or less advance warning of their flight. The quality of life depends on each camp. There are so many dynamics at play. Refugee camps are small—and in some cases large—towns of people who've been forced together and they have to redefine who they are in these spaces. Camps are usually in remote parts of the country and, depending on proximity to the border, can be very unsafe."

It was from such a camp that John departed for Canada and to such a camp that Sandra reluctantly returned, holding tight to his promise to bring her with him as soon as he could. There have been many similar partings in Africa and most end unhappily. At Edmonds, there are several women who were separated from their husbands—and, in some cases, children—in the refugee camps and have spent years fruitlessly trying to bring their spouses to Canada. But John had made a vow to bring his wife and unborn child over as soon as he could and, despite the odds and the difficulty, he kept his promise. "It was 2004 when my husband left and he was as good as his word," Sandra beams. "As soon as he arrived in Canada he started the process, saved his money, and sponsored us. We came to join him in 2005, and we have never left each other's side since."

Sandra still cries, but there is joy in her tears now as well as sadness. "This is my story of being in a war, of being a refugee. It's a terrible thing, so terrible for everyone but especially for the children and the women. I was a little girl when the war started and a woman when I finally found safety. In those in-between years, I lost my youth and my innocence. Sometimes I still cry, you know? Sometimes I feel guilty that I'm alive, that maybe I shouldn't be here and that it isn't fair I survived while so many others didn't. But then I remember that the Lord saved me so that my child could live."

Sandra's daughter did live and is now a student at Edmonds. Although her mother doesn't want to have her child's name published, she is growing up happy and healthy and is receiving a good education. As is often the case with refugee children, she had some learning difficulties to overcome, but with time and additional support, she is succeeding, and her future looks bright. Both Sandra and John are committed to bettering themselves through education and hard work, and to building the best possible home for the child for whom they've sacrificed so much.

Despite all of the damage that war has inflicted upon women such as herself, Sandra insists, "I'm going to be a success, and my child and my husband will be proud of me. Nothing and no one can stop me. I'm a survivor and I'm going to do great things."

8

A GUEST OF THE GOVERNMENT OF IRAQ

The Byrne Creek Library, the same place I'd heard Luc's amazing tale of survival several years ago, was full of school district and community dignitaries who had come to the school to select the winning projects in the Byrne Creek History Fair. Every bit of table space was covered with poster boards beside which stood well-dressed, nervous students waiting to talk about their projects—invariably well-crafted posters about their countries of origin. The projects were brightly coloured, with text, maps, and family photographs adorning the boards. They, and the students who had created them, were a vivid symbol of the school's multicultural student body.

One of the best posters belonged to Ahmad's teenage

daughter, Amira.* It was a remarkable display, crammed full of photographs and information about the history of Iraq. Amira beamed proudly as each judge, in turn, praised her for her hard work. It was indeed a terrific poster and she was justifiably proud of her work, but for me two things in particular stood out.

First, her poster was mere metres away from that of a student from Iran—a country that had been a bitter enemy of Iraq's in a futile battle in which the blood of hundreds of thousands of young people had been shed. Yet here, in the library of a school ten thousand kilometres away from the Middle East, two students from these countries talked easily to each other, the only thing at stake between them being a place in the regional history fair finals.

Second, and perhaps more important, was what was missing from Amira's project. While the poster hinted that there had been problems for her and her Kurdish family in Iraq, it didn't come close to explaining the almost unimaginable horrors that her father, Ahmad,* had endured in the country of Amira's birth before he fled to Canada with his wife and children—horrors he had suffered at the hands of his own compatriots. That story, it seemed, was for Ahmad to tell himself.

Ahmad is not his real name, and he has asked for anonymity. Despite the relative peace established since the American occupation, the situation in Iraq is still such that loyalists to Saddam Hussein and others who oppose a peaceful, democratic Iraq would disapprove in the harshest of terms of his decision to share his story. Ahmad knows first-hand how Saddam's followers demonstrated their anger in the past and doesn't want his children, or his family still in Iraq, to face repercussions. But still, he says, as justice and peace slowly return to his country, it is important that the world hears and knows just what happened to him and to the millions of other Kurds who died, suffered, and disappeared in the silent genocide of Saddam's Iraq.

"I was born in the north, the son of a wealthy man who died when I was young," he begins. "My father left us enough money for my older brothers to continue their schooling until the eldest, some twenty years older than me, was able to move the family to Baghdad where my oldest brothers found work and supported the rest of us and our mother." For Ahmad, life in Baghdad in the 1960s and 1970s was uneventful and, despite the absence of his father, the family prospered. After high school, Ahmad went to engineering school, completed both his undergraduate and master's degrees and, by 1980, was building a career as a respected young civil engineer.

"I had an excellent job," he says. "Thirty years ago I was making the equivalent of two thousand US a month, and I was able to travel on vacation to Europe whenever I wanted. I went to London, Poland, so many places." But despite the prosperity and peace on the surface, deep currents of unrest and violence were already ripping Iraq apart and would soon engulf Ahmad and his family.

Iraq is not just any country. It is a land with a tradition of scholarship and achievement going back five thousand years. At times it was an imperial centre itself, and at other times foreign empires coveted and fought over it. The ancient kingdoms of Sumer, Assyria, and Babylon stood on its soil. Alexander the Great conquered it, and Persia and Byzantium battled for control of the strategic region. From

Baghdad, the caliph ruled over a vast empire, and medicine, mathematics, philosophy, and poetry flourished there during Europe's Dark Ages. Later, the Ottomans held Iraq as a jewel in their imperial crown, until the British moved in after the First World War. Few places on earth have such deep roots in the bones of this planet. Indeed, the very foundation of Western civilization was set down in the area between the Tigris and Euphrates rivers.

The history of modern Iraq reflects that of its ancient counterpart. It is a history of revolution and military coups, war and invasion as citizens and foreigners alike struggle to control the wealth buried beneath the desert sands. Today, nearly 100 years after the first oil company started sinking wells, there is still an estimated 150 billion barrels left in the ground, with perhaps another 100 billion still waiting to be discovered. At $100 US a barrel, there are 25 trillion reasons to want control of the country.

In Iraq, just as in Sudan, there exists an explosive mix of oil and religion—and, though no less bloody, the factors here are more complex. In a relationship similar to the antagonism between Catholicism and Protestantism in some parts of the world, the schism between Sunni and Shi'a (the main branches of Islam) has long been part of the country's fabric. But the problem is further compounded by the presence of the Kurds (a non-Arabic minority who belong to both branches of Islam), the almost one million Christians, a small Jewish population, and the Ma'dan (the Marsh Arabs of southern Iraq with historical and ethnic ties to Iran and not Baghdad). For most of Ahmad's youth, these tensions were kept in check, by and large, by the ruling Baath Party. Pan-Arabic, socialist, tolerant of minorities, and secular, Iraq under the mostly Sunni Baath Party was far from democratic, but it was relatively peaceful. Then in 1979 Saddam Hussein, a rising power in the party, murdered his rivals, became president, and let loose the genies of racial hatred and war that would spread across Iraq for the next thirty years.

The troubles began, Ahmad recalls, with the expulsion of Baghdad's leading members of the Feyli, a subgroup of Kurds with a strong historical and economic influence on the city. But that was far from the end. In September 1980, after a long history of border disputes and hostility with Iran, Hussein ordered his troops across the border, launching one of the longest and bloodiest wars of the twentieth century. "When the war with Iran started I was doing well, but I started to worry. I was a Kurdish Shi'a—and, since Saddam liked neither the Kurdish people nor the Shi'a Muslims, if you were both you knew he could hurt you two times over. But still," Ahmad says, "I'd done nothing wrong and I thought I would be okay."

Two years later, Ahmad was in England on vacation when he was offered an engineering job. "The English were prepared to pay me two hundred pounds a week, but I turned it down," he says. "I had a good position in my own country and wanted to serve my people, so I returned home." Coming back to Baghdad would prove to be a very fateful decision. Between the police, the army, and the intelligence service (the feared Mukhabarat), Iraq was a country with almost limitless resources available to ferret out enemies of the state—real or otherwise.

On March 31, 1982, not one month after Ahmad had returned from England, Saddam Hussein made it clear that he very much considered Ahmad and the rest of his family a threat to the security of Iraq. "The security forces came to my house at midnight," he explains. "I was living with my mother, brothers, sister, and my brother's family. There were children living there as well, and one of my brother's wives was pregnant. The men knocked on the door, came in, and told us we had five minutes to get ready. We were put into cars and driven away. To this day, I have never seen that house again. It was a good house, a large house. It was ours, but we could take nothing with us—not even the photos of my dead father."

The frightened family was taken to the headquarters of the security forces, where dozens of other families huddled together. The women and children were soon separated from their husbands, brothers, and sons. Though the men were assured they would see their families again soon, few people dared believe it—and for good reason. In short order, the men were herded together and delivered to the first of several jails, places where they would live and die over the next six long years.

"First we were moved to this place, this normal house on Falastin Street in Baghdad," Ahmad begins. "Normal except for the maybe four hundred men and youth crammed into it." It was after two young men tried to escape from that first jail that conditions at the house worsened for those who were left. Torture and humiliation became commonplace. Eventually, the conditions were too much for Ahmad. Two months before, he had been a proud, patriotic, well-educated free man and the juxtaposition, the shocking contrast between his promising past and doubtful future, nearly broke him. "I cried," he freely admits. "I couldn't control myself and just wept. I asked myself, 'Is this really happening? Can people really do this sort of thing to others?' That day I thought it would have been better to have been killed."

But worse was yet to come. In August 1982, with the mercury hovering around fifty degrees Celsius, the men were packed into the back of transport trucks with furnaces blasting heat inside, and moved once more. After a seemingly endless ride, the trucks stopped. But the relief that the prisoners felt at reaching their destination and getting out of the trailers was quickly tempered by the realization that they'd been transported to Al Fathalea Jail, a notorious detention facility on the outskirts of Baghdad, a place where Ahmad and the others would be warehoused and forgotten by the outside world for one long year. Al Fathalea, however, turned out to be little more than a rest stop on a nightmarish journey, one that got worse with each successive move.

In Abu Ghraib, "the place of ravens," death was common—whether by firing squad, the gallows, beheading, electrocution, or other more horrific means, including acid and poison—and torture was routine. Ahmad, along with some four thousand other men, women, and children, was housed in this nightmarish place for a year and a half. Then in 1986 he, along with the others who had survived these horrors, was moved to Nograt Al Salman, a prison hidden deep in the desert wastelands of southwestern Iraq.

"There were no large walls at Nograt Al Salman," Ahmad says, describing the prison, "just these buildings in the sand. Many of the men and boys interned here had been at Abu Ghraib with me, and I knew them well." Guards would randomly come into the halls, which each held some three hundred prisoners, read a few names from a list, and take those people out to be tortured. If they returned, broken and bloodied, the next morning, their fellow prisoners—especially the doctors—could do nothing to help them for fear of becoming the next victim.

When he reflects on those days, Ahmad often thinks of a doctor, a man whose life and death symbolizes the tragedy and violence of Saddam's reign. "In that prison we were educated people—doctors, lawyers, engineers, businessmen, artists, and college students—and we were friends, brothers for one another in these jails. We lived together, ate together, and became family. I had this friend, a doctor, and I shall never forget him; he was such a remarkable man. He'd graduated from university in Baghdad, third in his class, and he was a writer and an artist as well. He would write these stories and poems and he could draw our pictures, in two minutes, with just a pencil. He would tell me stories about his life, and I would tell him and the others about my trips to Europe, and these stories would sustain us in prison. And then they took him, this man, this beautiful, innocent man, and they killed him. For no reason, no reason at all."

By late 1987 more and more names began to be called. "The guards started to take about a hundred people a week. The men and the youths named would go with them and we'd never see them again. But we heard what happened. Some of our friends were used as experiments for chemical weapons, while others were taken to the Iranian border, where they were forced to clear landmines with their bodies. These men would walk until they stepped on a mine. The mine would explode, the man would explode, and Saddam had one less mine and one less Shi'a or Kurd to worry about. This continued for months, a hundred men per week and, by the time Saddam gave us amnesty in 1988 to mark the end of the war with Iran, more than three thousand of us were gone."

The twenty-two years that have passed since his release disappear when Ahmad remembers those days and, despite efforts to control the raw emotion, his eyes redden and his voice quakes. "My brother and I survived," he says softly, "but so many others are just gone. And that whole time I never saw a lawyer, was never charged with anything, was never taken before a judge, and was never told my crime. That whole time I saw no one but my fellow prisoners and the security forces. We were survivors of a genocide and when they let us go, they said simply, 'Well—that's it. Go away and don't ask about your houses or your possessions; don't ask about anything. It's all gone, so don't ask because if you do you'll find yourselves back here.'"

Upon his release, Ahmad's thoughts went toward his family, the women and children whom he'd last seen nearly six years earlier. The news was bittersweet. They had spent some months in jail and then, in the middle of a bitterly cold winter, they had been dropped off close to the Iranian border. After a twenty-hour-long walk, during which many had died, Ahmad's sister and her family found shelter in Iran. Unfortunately, the journey compromised his sister's health and later she had collapsed and died.

Despite his years of imprisonment and the loss of his sister, Ahmad slowly pulled together the threads of his old life and started again. "I had to rebuild and so, in 1988, once I was out of prison, I started looking for work. I was very happy when my old company took me back, but I'd been away for six years or so and of course I hadn't worked and had to re-certify as an engineer. I also had to ask for a letter from the security forces confirming where I'd been and why I hadn't been working. So they sent the Engineers' Union a letter explaining I'd been 'a guest of the government of Iraq' in those years. A guest," Ahmad says bitterly, "maybe, but a very unwilling one. In any event, I saw my file at the Engineers' Union, opened it, and there I found that letter. Nobody was around and so I quickly copied it and put the original back before anyone knew I'd seen it."

Years later, that copy would prove to be very beneficial. In the meantime, his concern was with work and family. By 1990 he was married, and he soon had two children, but the shadow cast by his days in Abu Ghraib and Nograt Al Salman was very long, and it now fell on his family. "There was always a worry the security forces would take me away," he explains. "We released prisoners were required to check in with the security forces at regular intervals and every few months I got a letter saying they wanted to see me, or there was a knock on the door from someone telling me I had to go in for an interview. I'd go to the police station and an officer would sit me down and ask me questions like, 'What are you doing now?' and 'What are your brothers up to?' It was terrifying. Before each visit I was almost certain I'd never see my wife and children again, and the nights before the interviews I would be physically sick. I didn't want to go, and my family didn't want me to go either because they also believed every time I went I wouldn't come back home."

For Ahmad and the other persecuted Iraqis, there was a glimmer of hope with the arrival of the Americans in January 1991. Operation Desert Storm—the military operation to liberate Kuwait from the Iraqi army that had occupied Iraq's small, oil-rich neighbour the year before—was met with cheers from many within Iraq, as was the subsequent invasion by US and Coalition forces. "We thought things would be better and we cheered when Bush the Father sent in his army. We waited to be liberated from Saddam and were so happy the Americans were coming. The Coalition had destroyed the Republican Guard and was coming to free us, but then they stopped and left Saddam in power."

The failure to topple Saddam and the subsequent unwillingness to intervene as he launched massive retaliatory strikes against his enemies was seen by many Iraqis as a deep betrayal, a betrayal that cost the lives of thousands. "After the war, Saddam became even more dangerous," Ahmad remembers. "He was like an injured wolf and wanted revenge on those in his country who had conspired against him, and so he killed and killed and killed. In his mind, you see, he won the war. He stayed in his chair and was still in power. He was building palaces and castles throughout the country, using the oil money for himself. He destroyed our country, our economy, and our people. He killed millions of people but still believed that he was the winner."

For Ahmad, it was time to get out of Iraq. "By 1995 it just wasn't safe for me, for my family, for anyone. I didn't want my wife and children to be scared all the time. But in order to leave, we needed passports, and they were very difficult to get. I went to the passport office, and the official asked why we needed the documents. I explained that my children were very sick and needed medical attention in Jordan. That wasn't exactly true," he admits, "but I needed a good story.

"The man then said it would be very hard for me to get my passport because of who I was, and that I'd need to put up some assurances to guarantee that I wouldn't leave. He told me to use my house as a security, but of course I couldn't do that because the government had taken it already! So I had to give them money—one million Iraqi dinars on the spot, plus I had to sign over more in the bank, and give them the receipt in order to get my passport."

But even that hefty price wasn't enough to get his family out of the country. It took a meeting with another official, and even more bribes, for Ahmad to obtain passports for his wife and children. Immediately upon receiving their travel documents, the family quickly boarded a bus for Jordan and freedom. "Once we crossed over the border, I reported to the UN and applied for asylum for myself and my family," says Ahmad. "I told them what had happened to me, told them from my heart what had occurred. The people who work for the UN, the ones who listen to the stories and investigate, are experts in reading people. They knew I was telling the truth. But I also had the letter I found in my engineering file, the one that said I'd been a guest of the government, and that was all the proof I needed."

The United Nations High Commissioner for Refugees accepted Ahmad and his family as refugees within just a few short months and, not long after, informed him of their destination. "They told me Canada would accept me, and I said 'Okay, I suppose we're going to Canada.'" But, even with promised refugee status, Ahmad would have one more frightening encounter with Middle Eastern security forces. "The Canadian process was slow," Ahmad remembers, "and for two years we waited in Jordan for our flights to Canada. Finally, the Canadian embassy contacted me and asked me to produce a letter from the Jordanian police confirming that I'd been good in Amman and that I hadn't caused any trouble. This was a problem for me because there was cooperation between the Jordanian and Iraqi intelligence agencies, and I knew there'd be no doubt the Jordanians would tell the Iraqis exactly where I was and that I'd been accepted as a refugee."

With no choice in the matter, Ahmad reluctantly complied with the request. "The Jordanians told me to be at a certain place by eight in the morning. I arrived and the policeman waiting for me ordered me to walk ahead by myself for some five hundred metres or so to this bus. I got onto it and sat down with the others. It had blacked out windows and we couldn't see where we were going, but I figured out quickly that we had been driven to the main police headquarters.

"This man, I thought maybe he was a servant or a guide or something, took me off the bus and walked me into the building, all the while asking questions. He asked me what I had done in Iraq and why I wanted to go to Canada. I told him my children were sick and they needed medical attention there and, when we got inside, I was told to sit down beside these two civilian officers and there I waited. Soon I was taken into another room to be interviewed, where I discovered the man who'd escorted me in, the man I thought was a servant, was actually a police officer and he was the one who was going to conduct the interview."

The questions were repeated and Ahmad's answers remained the same. But he became very alarmed when the police officer asked him if he could prove that his children were really sick. He hadn't expected this line of questioning. After all, permission to go to Canada had already been obtained and the purpose of the visit was merely to confirm his good behaviour in Jordan. "I gave that police officer the name and number of our doctor in Iraq," Ahmad says. "He was an ear, nose, and throat doctor who'd treated our children back home for some things, and then this Jordanian police officer actually called him to confirm that my children were his patients. Then he took me back to the waiting room."

The interview took place around 10:30 AM and, by late in the afternoon, no one had come to see him, to follow up, or give him the letter the Canadians had requested. "I was still stuck in that waiting room," he says, "and I didn't know what to do, so I looked around and found someone who worked there and asked what was going on. But still, nobody told me anything." The waiting continued until well past seven in the evening, when an official came in and told him that he could now leave. With little ceremony, Ahmad was led out of the police station and sent home. "I was terrified and my wife was very worried as well," Ahmad says. "She'd thought that maybe I had been taken back to Iraq."

The Canadian embassy must have received the requisite letter because, not long after his interview, in April 1997 Ahmad and his family finally left Jordan for their new home. "We arrived in Halifax, Nova Scotia," he smiles, "but we lasted just a few weeks there. It was too rainy, too snowy, and too cold and so we moved to Vancouver, where we still are."

Ahmad is happy to be safe, but his thoughts and his emotions are mixed. "I had a normal life, a good life in Iraq. We came here because of Saddam, and if it wasn't for him we never would have left. He destroyed my family, my life, and my country."

Ahmad and his family are among those who have successfully connected themselves to their new home. His children have done well both at Edmonds, where they first attended, and Byrne Creek, graduating with excellent grades. Though there have been many struggles, he and his family have done better than many and he is immensely proud of his new nation. “When I received my citizenship in Canada, I was so happy. I told the government official that this day is now my birthday, this day I am really free.”

With three children already at Edmonds and a fourth on his way within two years, Latifa Jawansheer is a fixture in the school. She was with us in Richmond for a track meet and cheered her son, Sajad, on to victory. We travelled together to the hospital when her daughter, Maryam, sprained her ankle skating. A loving, dedicated mother and a valuable member of the school community, Latifa is always there to support her children. She is also a woman with a remarkable life—a story she shared with me for the first time several months ago.

As we sit and talk in my office, Latifa exhibits the poise and passion that was evident even before she became one of the first parents to agree to share her story with me. As she speaks in her soft, musical voice, the memories of her childhood fall from her mouth like poetry, like the yellow autumn leaves that dropped gently to the courtyard stones of their house in Khosal Mina on the west side of Kabul—a brick house with a tile roof the colour of clean winter snow, surrounded by thick blue walls.

Latifa remembers her grandfather, Mohammed Akbar, who would plant their garden each year on the second day of spring, a garden that, by the heat of August, smelled of fruit, flowers, and spice, a garden that provided them with so much food they seldom went to the bazaar. She remembers waking early in the cool of the morning, rising with the sun and the mist that floated gently over the spring that bubbled up in their yard. She remembers its water, so sweet and cold that people would come from all over the city to taste it. She remembers making the strong, sweet black tea her father loved, and spreading the blanket on the cool tiles and stone of their courtyard where she would lay out the baked bread, dried fruit, and eggs of their family breakfast.

Latifa remembers listening to tapes of the blind imam, Qari Barakatullah Salim, singing verses from the holy Qur'an in the solitude of those mornings and feeling deeply, reverently, impossibly close to God as the *azaan*, the call to prayer from the minarets, echoed across the city. And she remembers the first frost of autumn, the old man her grandfather hired to sweep the fallen flowers that littered the courtyard, and the sight of her brothers on the roof of their house, their kites rising and floating across the cobalt winter sky, straining against their frost-crusted strings.

Latifa also remembers the Russians and the stink of

their tanks as they rolled down the busy street in front of their house, the barking of their strange language. She remembers the sound of gunshots, near and in the distant hills, and she remembers hiding from the soldiers, believing the whispered stories of rape and death—stories made true a thousand times over. The Afghanistan of Latifa Jawansheer's childhood was also a place of violence, death, and occupation.

"I was born March 14, 1977, in Kabul and the first thing that I remember is the war. My family was wealthy by Afghan standards, and my father, Mohamed Hasham, was an engineer who served in the army. He was often not at home and we were left in the care of my mother, Jamila, and my grandparents." The third of nine children, Latifa spent most of her childhood behind the thick walls of their home and, though war raged outside, within she played games with her siblings and friends and helped her mother and her grandmother Maryam with the chores. In 1986, when she was nine, she started school.

"On that first day, I cried and said that I wanted to go home. But my father looked at me and said that I wasn't a little child anymore; I was now a big kid and it was my job to go to school, and that was it. No argument. So I went and learned different subjects like Math, Grammar, the holy Qur'an, and Islamic studies. When I was in Grade 7, I started to learn English. I would also go to summer school and study French and German. My mother was a nurse who had done her studies in French, and she wanted me to learn that language as well."

Education was of paramount importance for Latifa's family, a priority made increasingly difficult and dangerous because of the ongoing and intensifying battles between the Russians and the Mujahedeen warriors who hid in the hills above Kabul and rained rockets down onto both Soviet positions and civilian homes below. "I would see the Russian soldiers running off to fight, and we would hear the tanks, and my grandfather would make us lock the door and stay far away from them. They were tough men, the Russians, not nice, and we heard they'd take the girls and the women and rape them. I was scared all the time."

It wasn't only women who had cause to fear the Soviet troops. "Once, as a child, I was in the hospital for my back," Latifa explains. "I was in a ward with a boy whose hand and face were very badly mangled. He was my age, maybe ten years old or so, and when I asked what happened he told me that one of the Russian soldiers had given him a battery for his electric car, 'a special battery,' the man had told him, 'a very good Russian battery that would last for a long time.' So he put it in his toy, and it exploded. It was not a battery at all, but a little bomb designed to hurt children."

In the mid-1980s, the Russians and the state army nominally controlled Afghanistan and its capital, but the influence of the Mujahedeen was everywhere. Armed and trained by the West and portrayed in the US media as heroes and allies in the shared struggle against the Communist aggressor, the Mujahedeen were seen by many as liberators. But the reality for Latifa and her family was much different. "This Mujahedeen man lived on my street and he would constantly lecture my grandfather about us girls," she explains. "He would tell him that school was no place for girls and that he should stop us from going. This man would bother my grandfather all the time, and we even considered moving, but this was our house and, besides, we couldn't afford rent anywhere else." And so, for several years, Latifa and her family lived in an uneasy peace with both their occupiers and their neighbours—until two separate events in the latter half of the decade conspired to change their lives dramatically and irrevocably.

"In 1988 my grandfather died. Soon after that, the Russians left, and bad things started to happen to us. One day, late at night, maybe midnight, when my sister was washing her school uniform, she saw a shadow moving in the courtyard. My father was home at the time, and he told her she was imagining things, but still he went to check it out. People had been knocking on our door, you see, warning him to stop sending his daughters to school, and he was worried. When he went out to the yard, he found a mob of maybe forty people trying to occupy our home, all Mujahedeen. My father approached them and said, 'Leave us alone. You are Afghan and I am Afghan, why is there a problem between us?' But they refused to go, so he said, 'Then do what you will but at least let me protect my children.'"

The men must have listened because Latifa's father was allowed to take his family and secure them away in a single room while the Mujahedeen went on a rampage through the house, destroying lamps, slashing pictures, and shattering anything that could be broken. But that orgy of violence was only the beginning. "When they stopped, they told my father that he had three days to find them each warm green winter coats. They also told him he had to give them money, three thousand Afghanis, and guns as well. To prove their point and show they were serious, before they left they beat him with the butt of a machine gun. His nose, his head, his arm—everything was soon bruised and covered in blood."

It was an ominous sign that the freedom and independence that Latifa and millions of other Afghans had dreamed of during the long years of Soviet domination would soon degenerate into anarchy. Not knowing what to do, her father sought advice from those whom he trusted. The advice he received was twofold. First, he should not give the men what they wanted because, if he did, they would never leave him alone. Second, they should leave their home right away because they were now a target and things were going to get much worse.

"Just as they promised, four of the men came back for the equipment they'd asked for and my father said to them, 'I don't have these things and I won't get them for you.' This was not the response they'd expected, and so they started to beat him again. My father just stood there, saying he couldn't afford to give them what they wanted, and all he had was his life and they could take it if they wanted, but that would be all they would ever get from him. Then they beat him some more and finally left.

"A few days later, a letter was left at our house telling my father that his daughters had no place in school and that he needed to take this letter very seriously. It was almost at the end of the school year when this happened and my oldest sister, Farzana, was about to write her final Grade 11 exams while my other sister, Beheja, was about to write her Grade 10 exams. Threats or not, my father wanted them to finish the year, and so he sent them to live with a relative to complete school. I was only in Grade 8, and my father didn't want to send me away as well, so he told the school I couldn't do the exam and then explained why. My teacher replied that, since my grades were good enough, I didn't have to worry about it and so I received credit for Grade 8 without having to write the final exam."

Between the beatings and the threats, which grew more intense and serious with each passing day, Latifa's father realized the necessity of following the advice he'd received and reluctantly moved the eleven members of his family from the only home they'd ever known into a small two-bedroom apartment belonging to a friend in a high-rise building in a different part of the city. The move was in part to allow his daughters' schooling to continue, but, two months into Latifa's Grade 9 year, the government decreed it too dangerous for girls to attend school at all. Crammed together with little to do, the family lasted just one year in the small confines of their borrowed apartment. When the desire for space, their own home, and the sweet water of their stream became too powerful to ignore, they packed their few possessions and returned to their house. Surprisingly enough, they found it unoccupied. The home-coming, however, would be very short lived.

"We hadn't been back twelve hours when our neighbour, this woman I'd known my entire life, came over with food and a message. She begged us to leave and my father said, 'Why? This is my house.' But before she could answer, we heard a noise from her house and saw that her sons, two brothers, were fighting each other with knives and then one stabbed the other. 'You have to go!' she screamed at us. 'They are killing each other over you!' I found that strange, and I didn't know why two men, two brothers, would do that. Perhaps they were arguing over who would take our property or perhaps one wanted us to stay while the other wanted us to go. I don't know. They were originally country people, but they were also Mujahedeen while we were city people, and there was a big difference between us."

With no choice, Latifa's father contacted her uncle, an officer in the airforce, who sent a truck for them and their things and found a place for them to live by the airport. They stayed there until 1994. The Socialist government of President Mohammad Najibullah, impotent without its Soviet masters and armourers, fell in 1992, leaving the country at the mercy of competing warlords and militias, including the Taliban. By 1994 rockets continued to rain down on Kabul, the schools stayed closed to girls and, with no end to the violence in sight and the very real threat that the Taliban would take over the entire country, sixteen-year-old Latifa and her family, along with millions of other Afghans, slipped through a mountain pass and across the porous frontier into Pakistan. The experience, she remembers, was shocking.

"Pakistan was very surprising—the people, the culture, the language, the lifestyle, everything—but still there was the influence of the Mujahedeen and the Taliban. In Pakistan we had to wear the chador, and we girls struggled with that. For example, my sister and I were taking a bus one day, and she tripped on the step and hurt herself because she couldn't see through the veil. I didn't like wearing it either, didn't like covering my face, and I wouldn't even put it on until the day a man came up to me on the street and warned me that my face had better be covered the next time he saw me because if it wasn't, he'd kill me. I told my father about this, and he said that he supposed I'd better wear it then if I wanted to survive."

In the 1980s and 1990s, hundreds of refugee camps had sprung up in the northwestern part of Pakistan to deal with the onslaught of Afghans fleeing both the Russians and the Taliban but, unlike more than a million of her less fortunate countrymen, Latifa and her family managed to avoid the camps and instead found a place to live in the city of Peshawar, something she would be grateful for when, in later years, her work took her into the very heart of these awful places.

"But camps or not," she says, "the Pakistanis still treated us very differently, especially Afghan girls like me who had been educated with a European style. They called us white birds, and when a Pakistani man would see a particularly good-looking Afghan girl he would also say, 'Look at her! That girl's as hot as a machine gun!' White birds and machine guns, that's what we were called in Pakistan."

In Peshawar, Latifa returned to the Rabia Balkhi School, a new version of the school she'd attended in Kabul, where she studied all of her old subjects, including computer science and English. By 1996 Kabul and the rest of Afghanistan had fallen to the Taliban and life, paradoxically enough, improved for the Afghan refugees in Pakistan. Many of the extremists who had imposed their harsh views on Peshawar had moved back to Afghanistan with the Taliban triumph, and there was, she remembers, a loosening of the strict interpretation of Sharia law.

When she was eighteen, Latifa graduated from school with both excellent marks and a desire to help her people, and so she submitted her résumé to the International Rescue Committee (IRC), an NGO committed to working with Afghan refugees in the camps. They liked what they read and called her in for an interview. It went well, and before long Latifa was offered a job. "There were many different sections and jobs in the IRC," she explains, "but I wanted to work with Afghan women and children, specifically to improve educational opportunities and public health awareness. In eleven of the camps around Peshawar, we supported one hundred schools. We helped pay the teachers' salaries, provided lesson plans and professional development opportunities for the teachers, and bought textbooks for the students. I loved the work. I really enjoyed it."

And there was a great deal of work for the IRC and the other NGOs to do for the millions of Afghan refugees who eked out a terrible existence along the northwest frontier. Summer in that part of Pakistan was hot and stifling. In the camps there was often no electricity, no safe drinking water, not much food, and only the most basic shelter. Even with international intervention, the conditions in the camps were barely tolerable. And they were often made worse, Latifa remembers, by the corruption and greed of local officials.

"Some of the Pakistani police commanders would cheat the refugees out of their ration cards or purchase them for less money than they were worth," she says, "but the refugees, especially the women and children, had much bigger problems to deal with. In one camp I knew of a woman with two teenage daughters. They were seventeen and eighteen, I believe, and this woman would provide them to Pakistani men for five hundred rupees a visit. How desperate must you be to prostitute your own children for the equivalent of six dollars US? I found out about it and brought the news back to the office. The girls had asked me for help, and I said I would try to do something. Back at my office we decided to provide a separate place for the girls to live and then we hired the mother as a servant to help tidy one of the schools we ran. We paid her twelve hundred rupees a month to clean classrooms, the headmaster's office, that sort of thing. It was more than the going rate, but we did it to stop her from prostituting her children."

Remembering those days and the terrible conditions of her people is hard for Latifa, who is now a mother herself. "It was the women and the children who suffered in the camps," she says, her voice breaking. "There was—is—poverty, disease, gynecological problems, and drugs in those camps, lots of drugs. At a place called Khusan, there was a camp with more than four thousand families and we suspected more than half of them had issues with drugs. It was the mothers, you see, and it was all because of the carpets. The women earned money making carpets and it is backbreaking work, sitting hunched over for hours, weaving, and making these tiny knots with their hands. They almost all had children, these women, and to keep them quiet and sleeping so they could make the carpets, they'd drug their babies, feed them marijuana seeds to sedate them."

When Latifa turned nineteen, she followed the traditional route of many young Afghan women and got married. "My marriage was an arranged marriage. I'd never even met my husband-to-be before I saw him at a beauty salon where I was getting ready for my engagement party. I was with my future sister-in-law and in walked these two men. One had blond hair and grey eyes and the other was dark. My sister-in-law looked at me and said that one of these men was her brother, my fiancé. I didn't know which one was to be my husband but I hoped for one over the other," she admits, "and I got the one I wanted!"

Latifa speaks easily about her marriage. "These things are done according to culture. Comfortable with it, not comfortable, it doesn't matter. It's what you do in Afghanistan. But in my experience," she asserts, "most of the marriages arranged in this way are successful. Mine is very successful. My husband, Ali Mohammad, is a very supportive man and very kind. I am so happy we married. He pushed me to succeed, and he encouraged me to continue my work and my education and so, with his support, I obtained a degree in Program Management from Preston University in Peshawar."

Along with work and school, Latifa and her husband soon had a family. "Within a couple of years I had a young daughter, Maryam, and a six-month-old son, Sajad. I was working for IRC in the day and attending classes at night. My husband would look after the kids when Sajad was very small, but when he was a little older, I took them to the daycare that the IRC had established for staff. Then Ali Muhammad, who is a pharmacist by training, went to work for a Dutch NGO as a site manager."

In the fall of 2001, life took another turn for the Jawansheer family, once again because of war in their homeland. "Because of the September 11 attacks," Latifa explains, "the US invaded Afghanistan, defeated the Taliban and, after a while, I was free to go back with the children to visit family. It was still a dangerous place, but at least we could go back. I wanted to move back permanently, to use the skills and knowledge I'd gained working with my people in the camps in Pakistan, but there was a problem. My husband could not return because of some family issues," she explains, "so it was time for us to make a choice about where we wanted to have our children grow up and we then decided to apply for refugee status."

"My sister had already gone to Canada," says Latifa. "She'd scored very high on the TOEFL tests and was offered a scholarship at Queen's University, where she studied business management before going to Vancouver. She had married my husband's brother, and they were now established, and so they were in a position to sponsor us through the Joint Assistance process. After eighteen months of paperwork and waiting, we got a letter telling us that the Canadian embassy in Islamabad wanted to see us for an interview. This was December 3, 2005. We waited some more and received permission to come on August 12, 2006."

Latifa vividly remembers the excitement and nervousness of those days. "There were three children now. We'd had another child, a boy named Abbas, who was two. We flew to Vancouver, changing planes in Hong Kong on the way. In Pakistan, of course, most women wore the chador, and so when my little son Sajad saw this Chinese woman in jeans and with short, uncovered hair at the Hong Kong airport, he was very confused and asked me if the person was a man or a woman!"

The flight to Vancouver was the first time Latifa had travelled with her family. "I'd flown to Nairobi for a conference on HIV in 2002 and to Switzerland a year later for a workshop on grant writing, but I'd never travelled with my husband and my children before and I was very excited." Their journey was quite uneventful by most refugee standards, but there was still a tremendous degree of nervousness when they finally arrived at Vancouver International Airport.

"We cleared customs on September 11, 2006, and went outside to wait for my sister and my sister-in-law, who had also moved to Canada. They weren't there to meet us but, by co-incidence, there was an Afghan woman sitting next to us on the bench. She looked at my husband, who is very distinctive looking, and asked if he was related to Nahid, and he said, "Of course! Nahid is my sister," and the woman said she could tell because they look so similar. She had my sister-in-law's phone number, and she called for us and we learned they were still in their home making a welcome dinner for us. They'd assumed we'd be hours in customs and were very surprised we got through so quickly. They were soon there to pick us up and take us back for a big party.

"For a while, we stayed at my sister's place. She had an extra bedroom and so we moved into it, all five of us, until we could afford our own apartment. My husband quickly got a job as a produce clerk at a grocery store. Like so many other professionals from Afghanistan, he is not able to work in his field, but perhaps one day he will," she says, echoing a sentiment felt by many other professional refugees.

And so they started to build a new life and expanded their family once again with the birth of a son, Jawad, now three years old. "We currently live in a two-bedroom apartment and it's tough with four kids. They're growing and need their own space, but it's so expensive to move out. We're on the list for subsidized housing and have been for four years, but we're hopeful that soon we will be able to have a bigger place."

With Jawad still too young to attend school, Latifa stays home to look after him but she still finds the time to continue her education. University education or not, many doors remain closed to her, so she has made the decision to return to school and get her BC high school diploma. She also continues her work supporting other Afghan immigrants and refugees, volunteering as a translator with the Immigrant Services Society of British Columbia, and working with Afghan seniors.

"I love my people," she says passionately. "They're champions. They've survived war, suffered from poverty, the loss of family, their children, spouses, everything. And they've started over from zero, some of them several times over. I have suffered some of the same things they have and can understand, and I help them connect to people who can help them with mental health issues so they can deal with the depression and isolation many of them live with.

"And I give them advice. I tell them to learn English, no matter how old they are, and try to be patient. I say that if they don't know something or they don't understand, it's their responsibility to ask, to use gestures if they have to, but the responsibility is theirs. I say, 'Don't be shy and don't be embarrassed. Canada is a good and helpful place.'"

Latifa has advice to share with those born in this country as well. "What Canadians need to know is that a person from another country, from a different culture, is mostly just like them. Understand, however, that newcomers will suffer from culture shock and need time and patience."

As for herself? "My biggest hope and dream is to live to see all my children achieve their own dreams," she says passionately, echoing a sentiment familiar to all mothers. "Maryam is in Grade 7 and wants to be doctor. Sajad is in Grade 4 and wants to be a cardiac surgeon, while Abbas is only in Grade 2 but knows he wants to be an engineer

Latifa and Sajad Jawansheer

already. I'm so proud of my ambitious children. And I also want people to know my story and to learn from whatever lessons I have learned in my life. In Afghanistan there is an expression, 'Writing is the planting and reading is the harvest.' I want people to harvest my words and to understand that, here in Canada, anything is possible."

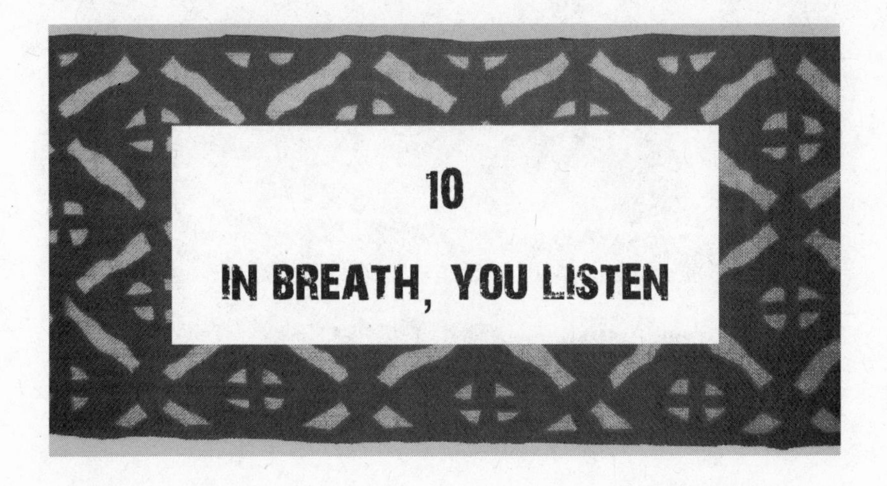

10

IN BREATH, YOU LISTEN

In my time at Edmonds and Byrne Creek, I have learned much about the true nature of education. I have worked with individuals who have expanded the boundaries of their jobs in order to meet the varied, and often complex, needs of our refugee students. These professionals have chosen to bring compassion into the workplace, to see the *whole* child (including the horrors of what has come before and the challenges facing the entire family in this strange new environment), and to embrace the creativity required to support these often-fragile students. In so doing, they have witnessed great successes and devastating failures, and each one of them has received gifts in return.

Dance teacher Shannon Tirling is one of these

professionals. Shannon has been at Byrne Creek since it opened its doors and, in those six short years, has built one of the largest dance programs in the province. Nearly 25 per cent of all students in the school take a dance class in the Byrne Creek Dance Studio, the nerve centre of one of the finest fine arts programs in the city. The most talented and dedicated of these students are invited to try out for the Byrne Creek Dance Company, an extracurricular club that Shannon runs before and after classes—a program which gives students the opportunity to continue their training and earn additional credits toward graduation.

Shannon looks exactly the way one imagines a dancer should. She is a wiry, slight woman, who is now in her early thirties. Originally from Victoria, Shannon began her lifelong dedication to dance at a very young age. "In dance, we breathe; in breath, we listen; and in listening, we slow down," she says. "And it is only then that we truly begin to hear."

The stories that Shannon hears are remarkable. Having worked with many refugee students at Byrne Creek, she has gained a unique insight into her students' lives. Along the way, she has formed a particularly strong connection with African girls. "I've heard repeatedly over the years that dance is a universal language," she begins. "I've even said it myself many times. But it wasn't until I came to Byrne Creek that I began to truly comprehend the depth of this phrase.

"Many refugees struggle in adapting to Canadian culture," Shannon explains. "Often they attempt to recreate themselves by assimilating to this new world while letting go of the past. Some try to erase it altogether while others attempt to preserve or hold on to their heritage. For my African-born students in particular, music and rhythm have often been deeply embedded within their lives, even before birth."

Shannon's gift is her ability to tap into the love of music and rhythm that her students possess. "Dance has the potential to impact these students immensely. Given that language is often a barrier for refugee students to communicate with other members of the learning community, movement becomes a voice for our vulnerable youth. Movement as a reciprocated language unites learners as the students come to see that intelligence is not determined by mastery of the English language. The confidence of our refugee students is built through dance. They can flourish within a community of mutual respect and acceptance."

One student in particular encapsulates Shannon's work with the school's refugee population. Nyalem Wan—a student with three siblings and a single mother from Sudan—is by nature the strong, silent type who keeps a lot bottled up inside. Nyalem needs to work evenings and weekends to help support her family, and she is responsible for much of the meal preparation and caregiving within her home. And so, despite her considerable potential as a dancer, training outside of school is not an option.

Shannon invites me into the studio to see what Nyalem is working on to give me a better opportunity of understanding the place that dance holds in this young woman's heart. When I arrive, I'm greeted by the strong, rhythmic bass of electronic music. The walls vibrate and the floors shudder from both the beat and the stomping of the dancer's feet. Shannon teaches all forms of dance—building from ballet and incorporating modern, jazz, hip hop, and traditional African movements—but the students are performing something I've never seen before. "That's Nyalem," Shannon says, indicating a tall Sudanese girl in tights spinning in the middle of the floor. "She's amazing."

It looks remarkable, but I have no idea what I'm watching. "They're bugs," Shannon explains as twenty or so teenage girls and one lone boy rotate and crawl upon the floor. "It's something I'm working on." She adds with a big grin. "I asked them to imagine themselves as bugs and then think what that insect would dance like. Watch this," she says proudly, "here comes the spiderweb part."

Shannon points out that what appear to be random movements are in fact very difficult, technically strong, and deeply rooted in traditional ballet. As the dancers perform *jetés* and *demi-détournés* and build up to the grand finale, she shouts encouragement. The music comes to a sudden end, and the students collapse dramatically into a heap on the hardwood floor.

As we step into her office, Shannon tells me more about her star pupil. "In Nyalem's first year in the dance company, back in Grade 9, when I asked the students to share something they loved other than dance, most told stories of school subjects, vacations, and food, but Nyalem spoke with a calm confidence about how she loves the rain. In Africa, she explained, rain is celebrated because it is so rare. That story is just so Nyalem. She is wise beyond her years."

According to Shannon, dance has given Nyalem a tremendous gift. "She was waiting her turn to dance, standing by the whiteboard in the studio, doodling, and when she walked away she'd written, "Dance because you have to, not because you should." That's why dance is important. It provides Nyalem with the opportunity to find out who she was in a way she never knew she could imagine. She feels she doesn't need to adapt and instead has been able to find her place without changing to fit into this culture. Her passion for movement and rhythm allows her to establish a Canadian identity without forgetting her history and roots. In our open studio space she opens up, reveals vulnerability, and builds strength. In dance, she is true to herself and has found success, pride, and self-worth."

Another professional who has chosen to extend herself so that students like Nyalem might find ways to forge their new Canadian identities without losing their pasts is settlement worker Leila Nemati. Along with her co-worker, Mambo Masinda, Leila has office space at both schools from which to do the work of welcoming immigrant and refugee families and students and helping them navigate their way through the system.

Like her colleague Mambo (who was himself a refugee from the Democratic Republic of the Congo), Leila knows what it is like to be a newcomer. Leila, her husband, and son came to Canada from Iran in 2006, after six years of applications, tests, and waiting. The Nematis were highly educated immigrants. Back home, her husband worked as an engineer in a cellular phone company, while Leila held a Bachelor of Arts in English, had substantial experience in the Iranian school system, and worked as a translator.

Coming to Canada was a risk, both personal and financial. They were both doing well professionally and understood they would be leaving their families behind, but the opportunity to have a new life in a free society was one they simply couldn't refuse. "We came to Canada," Leila explains, "started looking for housing and work and, although we'd checked out everything on the Internet, the reality was quite different. We thought we could speak English," she laughs, "but compared to the natives? Oh my God! I quickly enrolled in ESL classes at Douglas College, while my husband signed up with some employment services to look for work."

Both Leila and her husband soon discovered that their Iranian qualifications were almost meaningless in Canada, and it was only through a significant amount of hard work, volunteering, and additional coursework that they were able to obtain jobs that reflected their education and ability.

Since 2008, Leila has worked for the Burnaby School District and, in that time, she has come to see that there are two totally different types of immigrant and refugee youth who find themselves at the doors of Edmonds and Byrne Creek. "First, there are those who come in with a good educational background," she explains. "Mostly they are the children of skilled workers. They have done well in school before, and they get a big shock when they enrol here and get stuck in ESL classes where they study basic English and essential math instead of physics, chemistry, and the like. This reality is not easy on them."

Leila goes on to explain that the children of these families very often face tremendous pressure from their parents and will often be judged against relatives who have graduated successfully from high school and are already attending university in the United States or Europe. Such comparisons can be dangerous for youths who struggle with English or find themselves falling behind, and many feel hopeless, helpless, and angry. Dropping out and going down the wrong road are constant risks.

Leila understands the challenges these students face.

"What I have to do for youth like that is have them look at the bigger picture. I explain to both them and their parents the differences in the education systems between Canada and their homelands. Then I try to stop the families from making those comparisons, and I also remind them that, because of the time it takes to learn English, it may take them two to four years longer to get the same degree they would in their homeland. But, instead of worrying about it, they need to think they will eventually have a degree that can get them work almost anywhere in the world."

The second group of students Leila works with have a much different history. "Refugee youth often have a very limited educational background. Theirs has been a long, hard way and they have faced war and other life-threatening situations. Once they arrive, they deal with financial, housing, and culture shock problems and are very often desperate to make money any way they can. Often, they will find a job at a fast-food restaurant or gas station and just forget about schooling."

There are substantial differences between these two groups of students, but Leila's goal with both is the same. "Again, my job is to give them a clear picture of the system and their possible futures. I explain that success here requires their full commitment. Nobody can make them study and, unlike other systems, there won't be any threatening or physical punishments from a school administrator for not doing their work."

Leila admits that many refugee youth—in particular those who arrive at sixteen, seventeen, or even eighteen years of age—feel there is little point in caring about school, since graduation in the traditional way is almost impossible and so they seriously consider dropping out. However, she reminds them to look at things in non-traditional ways. "Education doesn't stop," I tell them. "There is always another way, always a chance to complete school if they have the desire. I also try to convince them that their future, if they stay at a low-level labouring sort of job, isn't bright. Those sorts of jobs are okay for a short time to help make a living, but enjoying a proper life requires education."

Leila is only one of the many staff members at the two schools who grasp the fragility of the prospects facing young people who come to them as refugees. Another is Wayne Best, a youth services worker at Byrne Creek. There is strong resemblance between Wayne and the movie character Shaft. Immaculately dressed, well educated, and articulate, Wayne has the deportment of a gentleman and the body of a defensive back. He coaches both the senior basketball team and the school's cricket team.

An immigrant to British Columbia via England and Barbados, Wayne is passionate about his job, which is to reach out to at-risk youth, to steer them onto the right path, and to help create a safe and orderly environment in the school. It's appropriate that he resembles a linebacker because he is, for many at-risk kids, their last line of defence between the straight and narrow and a life of violence, crime, and drugs.

In his time at Byrne Creek, Wayne has learned a lot about youth, in particular the challenges facing immigrant and refugee students. "Most kids, no matter what their background, turn out fine," he says, "and the refugees are pretty much like the other kids in many ways. But there are some key differences. With them, there are more stories. They've had harder journeys and certainly they're not so quick to extend trust.

"But, then again, why would they be?" Wayne asks. "After all, many of these kids come from places where authorities on a regular basis abuse their powers, and they can be quite skeptical of people in positions of authority. Boys especially seem to have more problems assimilating. Girls tend to find their way easier, it seems to me—at least academically. It's also much easier for the girls to get engaged in extracurricular activities, whereas the boys are more likely to find themselves out there somewhere, unable to connect, and they sometimes find themselves in situations where they make some bad choices and make friends with some nefarious people."

I'm meeting with Wayne on this particular day because we need to strategize about something that has come up that affects a family we share between the schools. I find him waiting for me in his office, flipping through the yearbooks of the last six years. He passes a book over and gives me updates on some of the refugee students we've worked with—some still in the school, others long gone.

For Wayne, it is an exercise in sadness and pride, success and failure. He points at a series of impossibly young faces. "That one's finishing up her university degree," he says, indicating a girl now in her early twenties. "Him? He's getting sentenced to armed robbery next week. That one's now muscle for a gang and, last I heard, he was running guns as well. This one's playing basketball at college. That one's working in a warehouse and doing very well for himself. And this guy? He's an up-and-coming DJ." The conversation is a sobering reminder that, despite the successes, some students still fall through the cracks and get involved with drugs, gangs, weapons, and violence.

The success or failure of students, according to Wayne, comes from a combination of many things: the degree to which they believe in themselves, their ability to deal with whatever demons haunt their past, strong family supports, their level of engagement at school, and their relationships with positive role models. "I see enough success to want to do what I do," he says. "And I focus on the positive. Like I said, most students—from whatever background, including refugees—will do just fine. But for those on the edge? If I can save one kid a year, I know I'm making a difference. One human being can make a huge impact, negatively or positively, to a lot of people, and I'll keep doing this as long as I can."

Like Wayne, Sarah Evans understands the significance of her role in the lives of refugee children. For the past five years, as Byrne Creek's English-as a-Second-Language (ESL) teacher, Sarah has dedicated her life to helping vulnerable newcomers and, along the way, has become a lifeline for the many refugee students who are committed to the education process. A multi-talented educator, writer, and businesswoman, Sarah has recently started a business aimed at supporting immigrant professionals. She has contributed articles to provincial magazines and has spoken passionately at conferences about the importance of education for refugee youth. Few teachers in the province have her level of passion, insight, and expertise. When I asked her to provide her perspective about what makes the difference between success and failure for a refugee student, she eagerly agreed.

"I've seen time and time again what a difference a few years make for refugee students," she begins. "If you happen to make it to Canada by Grade 8, life is significantly easier. I firmly believe that this is because learning requires some degree of emotional stability. Such stability is understandably lacking in the lives of impoverished and traumatized refugee newcomers, and a handful of very self-aware refugee students have confirmed for me that it can take several years to reach the place where learning can be successful."

"I recently had a particularly heartbreaking talk with a Grade 12 student who told me that he'd spent his first two years in Canada being immensely angry at having to leave his war-torn home country," she says. "He was really struggling with the realization that his time at school was almost up, and he was unsure how he would continue studying and working. This is often when reality hits home for refugees: when their non-ESL peers begin preparing for university while they start looking for work that will support their families."

Sarah readily agrees that the challenges of supporting older refugee students are profound. "It's exceptionally difficult for refugee students who arrive after Grade 10," Sarah asserts. "Many come with nonexistent or severely disrupted first-language education and very limited English. Some have no idea how to even hold a pencil. It takes time to navigate the basics of what school is about, and it takes even longer to recognize that the survival skills you previously relied on have become a detriment. For example, I've often noticed that newcomer refugees will hoard things, compulsively taking the whole box when invited to take one pencil or eraser. The initial transition period is particularly intense," she adds, "and I think this explains why beginner classes full of refugee students feel as if they have the chaos and energy of sixty students even though they are usually capped at ten or less."

Sarah has seen her share of heartbreak at the school. "A student of mine was recently suspended for fighting," she recounts emotionally. "He told me that, during the incident, he'd tried to use his words first, but he realized he didn't have any 'good ones' and so he punched the other student who was cleverly mocking him in front of everyone. Days after, when he brought up the subject, he told me he was adamant that he'd seen enough violence in his life and had wanted to walk away from the conflict and was genuinely saddened by his constant inability to do so."

The story Sarah recounts may seem tragic, but she insists that it is exactly the sort of thing that inspires her. "Working with these students, I see their immense desire to change and their ability to understand a depth of human emotion unreachable for many. I see that, although they obviously struggle more than other learners, there are many benefits to that struggle." Sarah has learned from her students as well. "They've taught me so much about the power of persistence. Rather than becoming disheartened, they accept where they are and rejoice in tiny pieces of progress as they inch forward—many of them carrying elementary picture books all the while talking of lofty postsecondary academic goals."

Sarah's relationships with some of her students have grown into partnerships. "In December," she says, "I was invited to speak at the British Columbia School Trustees Association conference on the topic 'What Makes a Student a Successful Learner?' I was asked to bring along a student who could share his or her perspectives on the issue. I wrestled for a while over whether I thought this was an appropriate request for an ESL teacher to make of a student. Most adults would struggle with standing on a stage, talking to a room full of several hundred people in their own language, never mind one they are still learning."

Rather than making the decision herself, Sarah decided to asked a student—a refugee from Iraq who Sarah felt could do a good job—if she was interested in speaking at the conference. The response was an unequivocal *yes*. "Watching her rise to that challenge and stand there with such confidence, poise, and determination to speak well was hands-down the most inspiring moment of my life," Evans says proudly. "Her speech began with, 'Let me tell you what I have lived through that has made me successful,' and when she finished, she was greeted by a standing ovation and many tears."

Sarah has found the right mix of pragmatic realism and optimism. She fully recognizes the challenges refugee students face, but refuses to let those difficulties stand as excuses for failure. "That girl's speech and the confidence with which it was delivered," she says firmly, "is the reason I can let go of some of my worry."

Another professional who recognizes the importance of confidence for refugee students is neither a staff member nor a parent. Besnik Mece is a former Albanian steeplechase champion, a high-ranking official in the Albanian Ministry of Culture, Youth, and Sports, and a track and field coach with thirty-five years of experience. He is also an immigrant who sees himself in the faces of the children of Edmonds Community School. With his wife, Tatjana, Mece has coached at Douglas College, UBC, and the New Westminster Spartans Athletic Club, and has made it a goal in life to provide athletic opportunities for disadvantaged youth. When he encountered a former Edmonds student with extraordinary talent (he is now in high school, a champion runner with the Olympics in his sights), and learned that the school had no coaching staff, he arrived at the school and offered his services.

At the recent invitational competition in Richmond, where Lois Madut performed so well, the fruits of Mece's labours were evident in ways far beyond the medals that Edmonds students brought home.

Four boys—Martin from the Congo, Junior from Liberia, and Sajad and Raez from Afghanistan—took their places in the blocks and waited for the starter's gun to begin the Grade 4/5 relay race. In a school full of good athletes, these four were in a class by themselves. Coach Mece had been working with the students since early February on baton passing and running techniques.

The boys were nervous, but they were also optimistic. Then they saw where they were running and confidence gave way to awe. The Richmond Speed Skating Olympic Oval is a magnificent structure of curved wooden beams and steel and, as the bus pulled into the parking lot, one of the kids looked out the window in amazement and said, "No way! We're gonna run in there?" The gawking continued as the thirty or so students and half-dozen parents scrambled off the bus and in through the front door.

With the race ready to begin, I was confident that the boys would do well. But I did not realize just how well they would do until the gun fired, and Martin exploded from the blocks. Within twenty seconds the race was over: Martin was fifty metres ahead of the next racer when he handed off to Sajad, who did his lap and passed the baton to Raez, who in turn gave it to Junior, who anchored the team for the final lap.

Latifa Jawansheer cheered loudly for her son, Sajad, and Junior's mother half-covered her eyes, afraid to watch in case her son might stumble or fall. He did neither, and by the time Junior, the fastest of the bunch, crossed the finish line, their nearest competitor had barely begun his own final lap. Edmonds had won by more than 150 metres.

To the chagrin of meet officials, Junior's mother ran out onto the track and hugged her son tightly, tears of pride falling from her eyes. "That kid's got a real future in track," a race official told me, but that was something Mece had seen weeks ago, and part of his plan was to expose Junior and some of the other children to those who could see their talent and potential—and do something with it.

I congratulated the boys and told Junior's mother how proud I was of him. "Me too!" she said, still crying. "I knew he could run, but I had no idea—none at all—how fast he really was." At that moment, I could tell his mother saw her son in a new light, as previously unimagined possibilities began to emerge.

Mece—like Sarah, Shannon, Wayne, Leila, and many others at Edmonds and Byrne Creek—are filled with imagination. They believe in the potential inherent in these young lives. And, though they do still worry, it is a worry born of experience, patience, and love. They have all expanded their understanding of what it means to work with students: not one of them limits his or her job (or volunteer commitment) to the confines set out by any standard job description. Instead, they have learned—as have I—that we are privileged to work with some of the most courageous and resilient children anywhere and that, for us to do them justice, we need to be willing to sit down with them, take a long, deep breath, and then, with all of the attention, creativity, and love that we can find, to listen.

11
KEEPING HOPE ALIVE

"I wonder sometimes," Mambo Masinda says as we sit and chat in the office space he shares with Leila Nemati, "if perhaps the soil has forgotten me." It's a good question for a former farmer like Mambo to ask. Mambo, one of the Burnaby school district's settlement workers, has always been a questioning, contemplative man. He is a man of principle and conviction as well—although at fifty-six he has conquered, or at least learned to control, the passions that governed his youth. It is right for him now, he says, to think about the rich, black earth of North Kivu Province, the soil that sustained his family for a hundred generations before, the soil that is as much a part of him as bone.

Today, Mambo's country is called the Democratic Republic

of the Congo, but it has had many names: the Congo Free State, Zaire and, in 1956, the year of his birth, the Belgian Congo—a colony slipping from the faltering grasp of its European master and stumbling toward independence and war. The bloody legacy of this independence would one day shape Mambo's life in a way he could not possibly have imagined, but as a little boy in the small village of Mambassa, a tiny collection of six families nestled between the forest and the fields of North Kivu Province near the border with Uganda, his mind was on other things.

Mambo was the eldest of eleven children, and his family grew by two when his father and mother, Kitsongo and Kavira, adopted two of his cousins who had been left orphaned when their parents died. Like millions of other Congolese, his was a simple life, dominated by family and hard work. "We had no electricity in our village and, because of the elevation, it could be quite cool in the mornings," Mambo explains. "Then it would warm up, rain in the afternoon, and grow sunny again. Birdsong from the jungle filled our ears in the day as did the sound of singing and drums at night. Darkness fell quickly in Mambassa, and we would be in bed by eight and up with the sun the next day. It was a pleasant place to grow up," Mambo adds, "although thinking of it always brings back confusing emotions and, when I look back, it's not always with nostalgia. But that life is part of me, and I will always remember the smell of the land, growing our own food, and watching the sun rise over the fields."

Mambo's life began just like his father's and grandfather's in all but one respect, and that was school. "My father understood the importance of education and he made sure we went to school," he says. "Indeed, most of the thirteen of us completed high school and two finished university"—no mean feat for the children of a poor farmer in a country where, even today, the literacy rate is less than 70 per cent.

"We didn't own our land," Mambo explains. "My father was a tenant farmer, working other people's fields, but he was an adventurous man and held different jobs to bring in money. At times he was a butcher, a truck driver's assistant, or a reseller of goods. He would travel far from the village, buy whatever merchandise he could, and bring it back to sell." His father's initiative brought in enough extra cash to allow Mambo and his siblings the luxury of an elementary education. "My first school was a simple mud building with a grass thatched roof and no electricity," he says. "Unless it was destroyed in the war, it's still there and very much the same. And, though it sounds like a cliché," Mambo laughs, "I did indeed walk to school barefoot."

When Mambo wasn't in class, he would spend his days working the fields with his family, all the while dreaming of escaping his small village and the farm, but never imagining just how far his journey would soon take him. Nor could he yet appreciate that the skills he learned tilling the soil—growing the peas, corn, and cabbages that sustained his family—would one day save his life in a dusty refugee camp. But all that still lay far in the future when, in 1967, Mambo's family left Mambassa and moved to Kayna, a town of one thousand people. Kayna was a metropolis to a boy who'd grown up on the edge of the forest, and there Mambo's father ensured that his schooling continued. And it was lucky for Mambo that it did, because the boy was soon to be presented with an unexpected, though desperately hoped-for opportunity.

Settlement worker Mambo Masinda

A teacher at the Kayna School named Solomon saw something in the young Mambo and took it upon himself to register the boy at Collège Pie X, a Catholic boarding school in Butembo—a red-soiled little city one hundred kilometres to the north. However, the teacher had taken this grand step without informing Mambo's parents. "When Solomon finally told my father," Mambo remembers, "he said, 'That's it. I've done my bit for your son and you can pay for him to go or not. It's your choice.'"

For a while, Kitsongo leaned heavily toward vetoing the opportunity, but he was eventually brought around to the idea by his son and his wife. "As I said, my father valued education, but he was worried that perhaps going away to school was excessive and a waste of money. Still, he wanted to support me, and so he let me go." But not without strings. Collège Pie X was not cheap, and the financial demands of a boarding school imposed a tremendous financial hardship on the Masinda family. "It took almost all of our income to pay for the school, and there was a great deal of pressure put on me," Mambo explains, "so if I went, I was certainly not allowed to fail."

Along with the prospect of higher education, there were other, less cerebral reasons for Mambo to celebrate his acceptance at Collège Pie X. He describes his father as a strict, authoritarian figure, and the thought of escaping his discipline greatly appealed to the boy. "But," Mambo adds with a rueful grin, "I was quickly disavowed of any notion of freedom by the priests at the school."

It was at the school where Mambo's passions for activism and justice blossomed. "I was a challenging student when I was fourteen or so," he admits. "I would confront the priests on behaviour, doctrine, indeed on the very notion of God, and I don't think they were very amused by this obstinate young boy from the forest." Though his grades were good and his intelligence noted, Mambo's behaviour drove staff to the brink, and he was very nearly expelled until, for reasons he still doesn't quite understand, he was given a second chance.

Mambo took full advantage of the opportunity and, by Grade 10, had settled down, was focusing on his studies and would eventually graduate with very good marks and a burning desire to continue his education at university. But that dream would have to be put on hold. "After high school, my dream was to go to university, but I also knew I had to obey my family, and my family told me that I had to help support them. Though I understood the reason, I was trapped," he explains. "I had brothers to get through school, and so I had to go to work. University for me would have to wait, but it was agreed that I'd work as a teacher until my youngest brother, Kambale, finished school, and then I would have the opportunity to attend university myself."

His decision to teach was no surprise, considering the influence of his greatest mentor in Butembo. "There was this great teacher at Collège Pie X, a Belgian by the name of Yves Everet," Mambo says fondly. "He was a man on the left of the political spectrum, and he would speak passionately to me about issues of injustice in our poorly run country." Under Everet's tutelage, Mambo began his career teaching French, math, and geography to Grade 8 and 9 students. But Everet also helped focus Mambo's passions toward social justice and political activism.

That idealism would be tested very early in Mambo's teaching career. "When I started working in the classroom, I quickly discovered that in the years since independence, the quality of education in the Congo had greatly diminished." Mambo also discovered that, if they were paid at all, teachers were not paid well. "I earned thirty-five zaires a month—barely enough to eat and pay rent. What little was left over, I sent home to support the family, as was the agreement, but we would go months sometimes without pay. Those were very difficult times."

By the late 1970s, more than just the Congolese education system was in crisis. Since 1965, the newly named Zaire was in the hands of Colonel Joseph Mobutu, the self-proclaimed "all-powerful warrior," a thug and robber baron with almost limitless wealth and infinite power who killed or jailed all who stood in his way. Unfortunately for Mambo, even though he was just an obscure teacher working far from the capital of Kinshasa, his passion for justice would soon have him labelled a dangerous enemy of the state, and his life would change forever.

For seven years, Mambo taught through the poverty and chaos in his country, as well as through his own personal disappointment. Through the many lows, he was sustained by the knowledge that when his little brother Kambale completed high school, his debt to the family would be paid and he could finally attend university. Unfortunately, it didn't quite work out that way. Kambale, it seemed, was even more passionate about furthering his education than his eldest brother, and instead of taking his turn supporting the family, he left for university himself, leaving Mambo in a difficult position.

"This situation caused great conflict in my family. My father wanted me to return home immediately and take up my family responsibilities. But, of course, I wanted desperately to go to university. This was the dialectic of my life: obedience to the family and following expectations while, at the same time, protesting against what I felt to be injustices. Also, by now I had developed something of a critical sense of thinking. This came from my mother, Kavira, I know. As an African woman, she had to obey her husband and family tradition, but she would still regularly find different ways of not following the rules. And I did the same all my life as well. I obeyed when I had to, but I always looked for an opportunity to break free."

Mambo found his opportunity one day when his father was out of town. Seizing the moment, Kavira gave him all the spare money she could find and, with that and his own scant savings in his pocket, Mambo left Kayna, quickly made his way to the nearest airport, and flew south to Lubumbashi in Katanga province. Upon arrival, Mambo enrolled himself in the university and committed to a degree in sociology, but his long-awaited post-secondary university experience wasn't quite what he had imagined.

"While at university, it became very evident to me why both the country and I had lost faith in education," he says. "There was no return on our investment. Education, it seemed, was the last priority for Mobutu's government—as if a quality education was a vestige of the Belgian regime. And we at the university wanted to change that." And there was much to change. Conditions in 1982, Mambo's first year at university, were abysmal at best. Many of the professors had left under protest, and the living conditions of the students were horrendous.

"How bad do you think it was there?" he asks me. "Imagine this. There weren't even toilets for students at the university. There were these ten blocks of apartments for us to live in, but there was also Block Eleven. That's the name we gave the section of bush beside the apartments that we had designated as the bathroom. When you had to do your business, you'd walk into that horrible place, full of excrement and filth and stench. These were the conditions the next generation of Congolese leaders were learning in, and it occurred to me at the time that Mobutu must have been preparing crazy people to run the country. These realties became the foundation of our protests."

He had come to Lubumbashi with the intention of studying sociology, but Mambo's real education would take place not in the classroom, but on the streets in violent clashes as the students began to protest against both their conditions and the president they blamed for them. Mambo remembers their initial rallies as disorganized and unfocused. "It wasn't as if we were actively supporting someone else against Mobutu," he explains. "It's just that we wanted other names on the ballots. We wanted choice and students wanted people to lead them."

The Congo is a heterogeneous mix of ethnic groups, languages, and clans, with loyalty to one's people, especially elders, valued above all else. The complexity of the country is mind-boggling and, in part because of its complex tribal makeup, Mambo became a leading figure on campus. He was significantly older than most of the other students (pushing thirty when many of the others were still in their teens) and soon was elected to represent his ethnic group, the Nande, at meetings.

"Tribal lines play a huge role in the Congo and sometimes some ethnic groups work hard to disenfranchise others," Mambo explains. "I was chosen to represent the Nande in conversations with the other clan leaders. For example, if I saw someone of my tribe marginalized, my job was to stick up for him and voice my opposition to that poor treatment. Looking back, I suppose I had some practical life experience, and I hope that I did my job with wisdom."

Mambo did indeed do his job with both wisdom and courage, as was evident in the tipping-point elections of 1984. "As usual, there were no other names on the ballot. There was only one candidate to vote for, but even then the election was not secret. You would go into the polling station and were asked what colour card you wanted. The voting cards were two colours: green and red. If you chose green, that was a public sign you voted for Mobutu, but if you chose red, it showed everyone present that you were against him. And, of course, Mobutu's men were all around, watching for those who took red."

Because of such overt intimidation, many Congolese were cowed into voting for their dictator. But Mambo, as a respected figure on campus and full of the courage of his convictions, knew exactly what to do when it was his turn to vote. "I had become a leader, after all, and so, when I went into the voting room, I took the red card. I could not in good conscience support the person we blamed for the pitiful condition of our country. Though my choice," Mambo remembers with sardonic understatement, "was not very well received by Mobutu's men in the room."

The students' conditions inevitably led to more, and increasingly violent, student protests. Mambo describes the way the students would make their way off campus in small clusters under cover of darkness, sneaking past the barbed wire and the army barracks, avoiding the searchlights, making their way downtown where they would reassemble in a mob of many thousands. "Our destination was usually the housing blocks in Lubumbashi where high-ranking government officials lived and worked. Our goal, as often as not, was to kidnap one of these men, to make our point, and to force change."

As he remembers the protests that shaped his youth and his role in them, Mambo's face clouds over. "A man will do bad things when he's part of a crowd of ten thousand. Sometimes we would achieve our objective and kidnap a government man. And sometimes they died." But the blood of more than just corrupt government officials stained the streets of Lubumbashi in those days. Often, the army had good intelligence about the student plans and knew when and where they planned to assemble. Then, like beaters flushing out grouse, troops would funnel the students down specific roads toward other soldiers who lay in ambush. "The army would wait for us with their clubs and sticks and guns. They fired live rounds, and you would see the people beside you shot. I don't know how I survived. It was a lucky thing, because you don't have control of the bullets coming toward you, and if you died then that was it. Your day had come."

Bullets were not the only things aimed at Mambo Masinda. His status on campus, his role in leading the student protests, and his actions at the polling station had brought him to the attention of the very highest levels of Mobutu's government. "After a while, I realized that I had become 'known' to the regime," he explains, "and being known by the president was not a very good thing at all." But Mambo didn't realize just how tenuous his situation was until word was sent by someone in Mobutu's government itself that he had been targeted for arrest. "Again, tribal identity is everything in Congo," Mambo explains, "and although the man who warned me was a member of the very government I was protesting against, he was also a Nande, and he had an obligation to look after me."

Mobutu was a dictator with almost absolute power, but there was still dissent against him, often from quarters the president would not have expected. "At great risk to himself, this man organized passage for me and a friend out of Lubumbashi. He told us to be on a certain train to the city of Kalemie at a certain time. We had little choice and so we went, but we still weren't certain if we were being set up or not, and I was almost positive we'd be arrested at the station."

The train carrying the two fugitives slowly made its way north, following the brown waters of the Congo River through forests, fields, and small towns to Lake Tanganyika and the port city of Kalemie, one thousand kilometres away. At every stop and turn of the track, Mambo and his friend looked anxiously for the soldiers they felt certain were waiting for them. But they weren't arrested and, upon reaching their destination, made their way to the home of a high-ranking army officer, a man they had been instructed to see by their benefactor back in Lubumbashi. "It sounds crazy that we would do this, but this man was also a Nande, and we knew if we were to escape we would need his help. Besides, we weren't sure if he didn't already know we were coming, and to not present ourselves would have been a mistake."

The officer confirmed that Mambo and his friend were being actively searched for by both his own soldiers and the police, and then threw a lifeline to his fellow tribe members by finding passage for the pair on a government boat bound for the town of Uvira, nearly three hundred kilometres to the north, near the border with Burundi. As the boat steamed through the blue waters of Lake Tanganyika, Mambo and his friend wondered just what they would do next. "Uvira would be a crossroads, I knew. I wanted to see my family very badly, but knew it was too risky to go home and, though my friend decided to take his chances and return to his town in North Kivu, I did not and I chose instead to leave my country and seek refuge in Burundi."

When the boat docked, Mambo travelled quickly north around the tip of the lake and illegally crossed over the Burundian frontier near the border town of Gatumba, where he presented himself to UN Refugee Agency personnel and begged for sanctuary. But things did not go the way he had hoped. "I also needed the Burundian government's permission to be in the country, refugee claimant or not," he explains, "and since they were friendly with Mobutu at the time, the Burundians very quickly made it clear I wasn't going to get it."

Mambo spent three months in Burundi fighting for asylum, but his persistence did little but annoy his reluctant hosts, who soon tired of him, drove him south to the Tanzanian border, and expelled him. His initial stay in Tanzania, however, was brief. "I was promptly sent back to Burundi by the Tanzanian officials," he smiles. "So I crossed the border, walked back into Burundi, and was promptly arrested. Burundi had made it very clear they didn't want me, so I was released once more, and taken back to the border. They took my papers and wrote a message to the Tanzanians in them. 'We've expelled this man twice now,' the Burundians said. 'You keep him. We don't want him back!' There was nothing else for the Tanzanian officials to do and so they relented and let me stay."

The Tanzanians sent Mambo to the Kigwa refugee camp in the central part of the country, where he would stay for the next three years. "There were four thousand or so of us at Kigwa, and it was a shocking experience for me. It was dirty and dusty, a place of scrub bush, tents, and wire. I spent my first night there in an auditorium with the other newcomers, and the next morning I was given a tent, machete, beans, food oil, and some sugar. Then I was left to fend for myself with the other Congolese, Burundian, and South African refugees."

At Kigwa, Mambo was housed with other educated asylum seekers. "We tended to be educated refugees in the camp, active in politics and protest. Some were students like me and the South Africans were members of the ANC. We were not peasants; we were people considered dangerous by our own governments." Mambo quickly realized that many men at the camp were dangerous for less philosophical reasons as well. Some had been in the camp for years and, in the craziness of the place, had drifted into illicit activities such as drugs, alcohol, crime, and violence. Mambo understood the fate of those who languished too long in the camps and began to plan his escape.

"I asked myself, 'What can I do to get out of this place? What can I do to stay mentally fit, to stay sane?' I could get no word to my family for help, or to even let them know I was alive. It was still too dangerous for them and for me, but I had to do something and so I turned to the camp director for help. There were two men with power at Kigwa: the local head of the UNHCR and a Tanzanian government official in charge of the camp. Of those two, I quickly learned that the real power rested with the Tanzanian and so I asked him for seeds—carrots, cabbages, and such—so I could grow fresh food to feed both my mind and my body. Fifteen years after I left the farm, I returned to my roots and, for the first time in my life, was very thankful for my farming background. Many at the camp didn't know how to look after themselves, to feed themselves, and so they suffered greatly."

For the next three years, Mambo tended to his small plot, supplemented his diet with fresh food, and sold the surplus to anyone who could spare a few Tanzanian shillings. As the months passed, he started to build up a small amount of savings, though for what he didn't know. This was, after all, a time of waiting for Mambo, stuck in what he poignantly describes as "a neither-here-nor-there place."

He wanted desperately to go home, but he was a marked man in Zaire and reluctantly realized that the next best thing was resettlement: "I did the paperwork to get out and my options were go to Canada, the United States, or Australia. Canada was my first choice since they spoke French there, and I figured I could handle that, even if it was as cold as I'd heard."

It took many years—and many risky undertakings—for Mambo to see his name on a list of refugees who would be accepted by the Canadian government. But finally, in March 1988, Mambo boarded a plane for the flight to Quebec City. Even now, he barely has the words to describe his thoughts and emotions on the surreal aerial hopscotch that took him from Tanzania to Quebec City via Amsterdam, Toronto, and Montreal. After years of struggling to survive mentally and physically within the confines of the camp, Mambo would journey almost thirteen thousand kilometres in three short days.

"It was March 4, 1988, when I and the other refugees finally arrived at Quebec City. I will never forget the reception waiting for us as we stepped off the plane. It was cold, very cold! When we landed in Toronto, we'd been given winter coats and boots so we would be properly dressed. I remember that, in Mambassa, we considered it a cold day when the temperature dropped to nineteen degrees centigrade—but it was much colder than that in Quebec! There was snow on the ground, the first time I'd ever seen it. But still, I hardly felt the chill, I was so excited. We were greeted by this man at the airport, this wonderful man, a government official, and though I can't remember his name I remember his face like it was yesterday. He smiled at us, shook our hands, hugged us, and made us feel like we were friends coming home."

Mambo's next twenty years in Canada passed quickly. He earned three university degrees, including his PhD, in quick succession. When he received Canadian citizenship, he flew back to the Congo to marry a woman from his hometown and adopted two nieces and a nephew left orphaned by the ongoing Congolese conflict. By 2005, the family had relocated to BC. Mambo took a job as a settlement worker with the Burnaby School district in 2008 and soon had office space at both Edmonds and Byrne Creek, helping brand new families adjust.

Mambo's skills at navigating the labyrinth of paperwork necessary to sponsor a refugee were once again put to use for his own family when, in partnership with his church, he started the process of sponsoring his parents Kitsongo and Kavira to Canada as well. He vividly remembers their arrival at the Vancouver International Airport in 2007. "It was a huge shock, but a positive shock for them. I mean, there they were arriving at the airport and there were us—as well as a team of white people, Japanese people, and Chinese people—all cheering for them. It was a celebration of the unity of humanity, and it was a blessing. I realized very clearly at that moment that we are all the same—black, white, whatever. Some people are bad, no doubt, but the world is also full of good people, very good people."

Unfortunately his reunion with his parents was a short-lived blessing. His mother died January 19, 2010, and his father passed away two months later to the day. "I suppose when two people live together for so long," Mambo says stoically, "that when one goes, the other is certain to quickly follow."

Mambo is still actively fighting for social justice, currently as a principal fundraiser in the Kasando Project, a non-profit organization working hard to build an elementary school in the village of Kasando in North Kivu province, not far from where he grew up. He has never forgotten the barefooted boy he once was, toiling in the fields with dreams of a better life. And he knows that the little boys and little girls of North Kivu today are no different than he was nearly half a century ago—full of promise, hope, and endless potential, waiting only for a chance. It is Mambo's greatest wish that he can do for these children what Solomon and Yves Everet did for him: provide hope with action.

The Kasando Project aside, Masinda continues his work with the school district, helping recently arrived immigrant and refugee families. In the space of one week, he helped register two little boys from Iraq, two sisters from the Philippines, and two children from the Congo itself, their mother crying with relief as he greeted her in her own tongue. Whenever Mambo welcomes a new family, his mind is always on his own welcoming on that cold March day in Quebec. "I think of that man who greeted me every day and smile when I see a new person. There is no price on that, but I know from my experience that a smile and a kind word from a stranger never leave your heart."

He has other advice for refugees as well, hard-earned

from very personal experiences. "We refugees come here with high expectations, and sometimes when they aren't realized, we can fall into disappointment, despair, and lose hope. But if you can keep hope alive and couple it with hard work and action, you will most likely succeed. Keeping hope alive: that, I believe, is the real challenge. Some people come here with dreams but fall into the cracks, no doubt, but there are many more who—with help, hope and action—can succeed."

And that challenge is one the greater community needs to take up as well, Mambo adds. "Know that most of us who have lived in a refugee camp have lost family, community, and country, so when we move here we try very hard to recreate our lives, but we need help with this, help to get connected to the community we move into. We all need to work together," Mambo asserts, because people who join forces and unite "will achieve far more than those who toil alone."

12
ALWAYS A SAFE HAVEN

It's an unwelcome sign of the times that the Friday morning lineup for food seems longer than it used to be. Inside the Edmonds Community Room, volunteers prepare the bags of bread, vegetables, and canned goods, ensuring that everyone sitting patiently in the hallway will get what they need to feed their families for a day or two. Doreen George, Edmonds' community coordinator, is flitting between the food line and the breakfast program, where staff members and parents are feeding more than fifty students a nutritious meal of bagels and cream cheese, milk and cereal. Doreen is keeping an eye on things and greeting parents and students alike with courtesy and respect. I make an appearance, but this is Doreen's show—and the thin, steel-haired Scot is more than capable of handling any issues that arise.

Community Schools exist across British Columbia. In essence, their role is to provide enhanced opportunities, through the school, for both students and other members of the neighbourhood. In some schools and districts, the community coordinator acts as a glorified booking agent, leasing class and gym space to groups such as the Girl Guides or private clubs looking for a space to play indoor soccer. At Edmonds, however, the role is infinitely more complex.

Under Doreen's leadership, the community component of the school has exploded. The school offers a clothes bank and a food distribution program and, in partnership with Immigrant Services Society of BC, provides space for an Afghan seniors' club facilitated by Edmonds parent Latifa Jawansheer. With a gift for getting grants, Doreen has found the money to offer a multitude of other programs as well. Edmonds runs a hot-breakfast program for upwards of sixty students a day staffed by several parents including Mehari's mother Wubet, has a partnership with Burnaby Firefighters to provide recess snacks, offers a program called Partners in Education—a parenting support program run by the Vancouver Canucks Family Education Centre—and, with other community partners, offers a wide range of athletic, fine-arts, and culinary programs for the children and families of the Edmonds neighbourhood.

Doreen George has no use for charity and will turn an icy Scottish glare on anyone who describes the programs she administers as such. "It's about empowering and enabling parents to help themselves, and to meaningfully improve their own lives and those of their friends and neighbours," she says. "Parent volunteers run the clothing room and assist with the food distribution. Parents run conversation and cooking clubs for other parents and more-established immigrants and refugees connect with newcomers, helping them settle and acclimatize."

Doreen George has done a commendable job of tapping into the resources and goodwill of partners like Costco, Telus, and the Lions and Rotary clubs, as well as individuals like Peggy Woodruff, who takes it upon herself to provide several thousand new books a year to the students. There are, however, several other people who have given thousands of dollars and hundreds of hours of their own time to the school. Hungry children can't learn, after all, and sometimes parents need support to learn new ways to cope in a strange country, but a parenting program is not the true focus of the school. Learning is, and at Edmonds it takes more work to create the conditions necessary for students to achieve academic success.

So how then does it happen? How do Mehari, Victor, Lois, and the rest of the 80 per cent of Edmonds students who came here speaking different languages learn English, settle in, and find success? How do we introduce them to the miracle of language, the gift of looking at a book and seeing letters and words that makes sense, instead of indecipherable scribbles? And, while we're busy making the school effective for the refugee and immigrant students, how do we also create an environment where the school's Canadian-born children have *their* needs met as well? Despite its unique population, Edmonds is still a neighbourhood school which offers all the other programs and curriculum expected from any school in the province.

According to Head Teacher Elin Horton, making it work for all children at Edmonds takes both a remarkable team of educators and a special way of seeing the world through the eyes of children. "The first thing a teacher here must do," Elin explains, "is develop the ability to see past whatever preconceived notions may exist." On this point, she is unwavering. "There are some children in the school who have a reputation for mischief, no doubt. But if you, as a teacher, think that they are just troublemakers or bad kids and that is as far as your understanding goes, you're never going to have any success with these children. But, if you care enough to learn what's happened to them in their lives and gain an understanding that these children have endured things you couldn't possibly comprehend, you very often come to the conclusion that, all things considered, they're actually doing much better than you could have possibly expected. Once you get that, the learning will happen."

There is also, Elin says, a realization on the part of staff that refugee children have pressures put upon them that the average student couldn't begin to understand. "Their families say things to them like, 'We've come here to Canada for you,' or 'you're going to school to save your family.' These kids take that sort of thing very seriously but, at the same time, when they're new they don't really have a clue what's going on and so they work hard and watch and try to figure out by the actions of those around them what it is they are supposed to do. They do this for six hours a day. It's exhausting."

Elin's years of experience at Edmonds have also taught her that building positive relationships with the parents is critical. It seems obvious, but when you factor in the language barrier, the nervousness of parents to trust agents

Pauline Wong, Maggie Lin, and Kiara Barracks

of the government—like teachers—and often their own lack of education, building bridges to the parent community can be more challenging at a school like Edmonds or Byrne Creek than at most. Elin, however, refuses to buy into excuses. "Point, sign, draw for God's sakes," she says, "and do whatever it takes to communicate."

To understand that there are expectations put upon you here that go far beyond the job description of a typical teacher is another characteristic of a successful teacher in a place like Edmonds, Elin adds. "Teachers here understand that, although they fill the traditional role that other schools do as well (teaching the curriculum of Math, Social Studies, Language Arts, and the like), they also act like a new and extended family. We've written letters to the UNHCR trying to get families reunited, raised money to send people home to visit dying relatives for one last time, and have helped people pay for dancing lessons and purchase prom dresses.

"Remember," says Elin, "It's about equity. You don't give everyone the same thing—you give each child what they need to reach the same place. And kids here sometimes need more from us to achieve that same outcome as other children. All our staff understand that, and the ones who've been here for years are exceptional."

Elin sits back and reflects on the school and the people she works with, rattling off the names: "Pauline Wong, Peter Agg, Andy Bigiolli, Marg Zarin, Karen Dawson, and Balbir Bains. These are teachers, cooks, secretaries, and custodians and each has a different role but no matter what they do these are creative, welcoming, and caring people. They respect the individual. They know that one size does not fit all and they constantly strive to learn. They figure out that there are things they don't know and work hard to learn them.

"This school will always be a safe haven," she says, "a place of miracles. Children will come here as they always have and be successful, and find their way in the world. And if I've had some small part of that, then I'm happy. I wouldn't trade a second of my time here for anything and I wouldn't work, couldn't work anywhere else. There's always something to smile about in this place.

"Like I told the Vancouver *Province* when they did a feature on the school a couple of years ago—we can't change where our students are from but we can do an awful lot about where they're going to go."

ENDINGS

Twelve years ago, on the dusty plains of southern Sudan, an Arab militiaman or perhaps a government soldier ripped a little boy from his screaming mother's hands and threw him to the ground. Bullets were expensive and a target so small and frail was not worth the cost of one, so the man flipped the rifle around in his hands and, for some senseless reason, drove the butt of the gun into the boy's head, leaving his little crumpled body to die in the sand.

At least that's what we believed happened to Akol Chol* from the few fragments of his story we knew. His mother, Mary, hardly more than a child herself when Akol was born, guarded her son's story closely, sharing it tentatively, piece by piece, with the few people in the school she trusted. What is known beyond doubt, however, is that somehow the little boy was grievously injured in the war waged against the southern "infidel" tribes by the government in Khartoum, which killed them in great number for the same reasons people in Africa have killed one another for centuries: land, women, water, cattle, and the proper name of God.

Fleeing Sudan for the safety of a refugee camp, Akol and his family were accepted by Canada and were flown to Vancouver—or at least what was left of his family was, for Akol's father had disappeared from the refugee camp, lost forever in the desert, leaving his pregnant wife, Akol, and his older brother alone in a very strange and terrifying new world.

Mary soon discovered that the streets of North America were not kind to frightened, lost Africans, especially a single mother with a child like Akol. Overwhelmed, mired in poverty, a third child on the way, and adrift in a strange country, she turned to the state for the help her son desperately needed, the help she couldn't provide herself, and voluntarily placed her son in the care of the Ministry of Children and Family Development. The social worker found Akol a foster placement as close as she could to Mary, who saw her son several times a week. Though they lived apart, the bond, always strong between the two survivors, continued to grow. That fall Akol, like thousands of other eight-year-olds across the country, registered for school with Mary at his side.

At the school and with physiotherapy, speech therapy, and intensive one-on-one-intervention, a small miracle happened. A funny, loveable little boy, tall for his age, and big, his short curly hair covered by a hard foam helmet—a hint of who Akol should have been—emerged from his wheelchair-bound shell.

The staff shared Akol's growing list of small victories. We cheered when he took his first few steps out of his wheelchair, the first time he kicked a soccer ball, and the first time he danced. And we also discovered his great sense of humour, which started with a cow. Akol loved cows, a genetic gift perhaps from his herdsman forefathers, and he had his own, a small stuffed version of the real thing. Little cow in hand, Akol would sometimes pull himself up from his wheelchair and amble down the hallway, waving the toy in peoples' faces, and make mooing noises to his own great amusement and to ours.

He learned to say "cool," to high-five his classmates, to throw a football, to use a pretend cell phone, and to type on a computer. He was a joker and nobody was safe from his pranks. At one of our assemblies, Karin Johnson, our music teacher, was leading the students in a song and a dance. The children were bouncing and singing around the gym when, to everyone's surprise, Akol broke out in song and joined them, stomping his legs happily to the music.

I sat next to him, and he soon noticed I wasn't singing. With no sense of personal space, Akol leaned into me, his eyes only a few inches from mine, and gave me a why-aren't-you-dancing look, and then kicked my leg. I started swinging my legs alongside his, and he roared with laughter. But when I stopped moving, the glare returned, and he kicked my leg again. The message was clear: if he could dance, then so could I.

Sometime just before the Christmas break, a commotion rose from the hallway outside the office. I stepped out to see a cluster of teachers and education assistants flock around a tall African woman in her mid-twenties, holding a little baby in her arms. The woman was Mary, and Akol was meeting his little sister for the first time. Suddenly I heard a voice cry "Mama!" from down the hallway. I turned to see Akol in his wheelchair being pushed toward us. Mary smiled, leaned down, and hugged her son. Akol was happy to see his mother, that was obvious, but his gaze was fixed on the little baby in her arms, a huge smile on his face.

"Sister! Sister!" Akol said again and again as he sat there, baby cradled in his arms, vibrating with excitement. When he was a toddler, Akol had been left for dead, his head split open by the butt end of a machine gun. He'd been severely brain damaged, could walk only for short distances, and knew, at best, twenty words in English. But we all looked in wonder at this beautiful boy showing more compassion and love than I'd ever seen displayed by anyone in my life.

Akol smiled, rocked the baby gently in his arms, and kissed her cheek. And then he cried, small tears falling from the corner of his eyes. "Sister," he cooed over and over again as Mary beamed and softly sang her children a lullaby. She had a beautiful voice, and I was to learn later that when Akol was younger and had seizures, his mother would sing him out of them, her soothing voice washing over the boy. It was a tender, achingly beautiful moment.

Three days later, we broke for the Christmas holidays and, when we returned, a panicked message from Wendy Hampe, the public health nurse who serviced our school, was the first thing that greeted me. It was about Akol, and I was to phone her immediately. Over the break, I learned, Akol had developed a terrible fever and had been taken to Children's

Hospital. The doctors found fluid on his brain and had immediately performed emergency surgery to drain it.

They believed that perhaps a sinus infection had spread to the scar tissue in his head and then found its way into his brain. I asked about the prognosis. Wendy was silent for a moment, and her response numbed me. Bleak. Akol was unconscious, in a coma, and if he woke up—and there was only a slim chance of that happening—he wouldn't be the same. He had a high fever, the infection was causing massive brain damage, and the antibiotics weren't working.

I ushered Elin Horton and Vice Principal Stephanie Miller into the office and gave them the news. Both cried for a while, but very quickly wiped their eyes and announced that there was work to do and the tears would come later. We called the aides down to my office to let them know and they stayed there for a few moments, crying and hugging each other while I went to get Akol's teacher, Laurie Copeland. I brought her back to the office and gave her the news, and it was no surprise her reaction mirrored Elin's and Stephanie's. I offered to call in a substitute teacher if she was too shaken to continue, but after thinking about it for a while, Laurie declined, stating that her place was with her students.

And speaking of the students, she wanted to know what to tell them. After all, Akol was overdue returning from the holidays and they were already asking about him. It was a good question. We hadn't even talked to Akol's mom, foster parents, or social worker at that point and, in an age of privacy, we needed to be very careful with the sharing of information. In the end, we decided to let them know just that he was sick and not able to come to school just yet.

We walked back to the class. Laurie had a couch in the

back corner of the room. It was Akol's; he suffered seizures and would be exhausted after one and need to sleep, so someone on staff brought it in for him to use. I sat, gathered the students around me, and told them Akol was sick and wouldn't be back at school for a while. Twenty sets of eyes stared intently at me. They loved Akol and were saddened by the news.

Mehari, one of his classmates, piped up immediately, declaring the class would make Akol a card and a tape of his favourite songs. Mehari had long ago declared himself Akol's best friend and spent his lunches pushing his friend around the playground. And then Mehari ran to his desk, rifled through the mess of paper, and with a small grunt of triumph pulled something out of it and handed me an old, beaten-up Matchbox car. At best guess, it had once been a Ferrari, but with the scratches, dents, and missing wheel it was hard to tell. He said that the car was his favourite toy, and he just knew that Akol would feel better if he had it.

And then we got to work. Wendy pulled some strings at the hospital. Children in such critical condition are normally only allowed immediate family visits, but with some convincing, the hospital granted permission for school staff to visit. Elin organized a duty roster of staff to support Mary: we took her to and from the hospital and babysat Akol's brother and sister. Ginny Tahara, the school counsellor, allocated several hundred dollars from an Edmonds-based charity, the Burnaby Children's Fund, and took the family shopping, loading up on food and diapers. Through it all, Edmonds staff continued to visit Akol at Children's Hospital. But not me. Not yet. As pathetic as it was, I hated hospitals and had not worked up the nerve to go.

True to his word, Mehari made the tape and it was a classic; he'd organized the class to sing a song. He told me it was a popular hip-hop song but, with most of the kids still learning English, I couldn't tell which one it was. Elin and Charmaine Calbick, one of the education assistants, took the card, the tape, and a picture of Akol to the hospital to show the doctors what he'd looked like before he got sick. They also took with them a large stuffed cow and placed it on the foot of his bed. Elin told the hospital staff the significance of cows and they promised to look after it. School staff also ensured that Akol was looked after properly, staying at his side for hours, and often overnight.

The next few days passed slowly. Life went on, but always in the back of our minds was a little ten-year-old boy, lying in a hospital bed, fighting for his life. I received regular updates from the hospital, and the news was never good. Akol wasn't getting better, the infection raged and, despite their best efforts, the doctors were unable to break it. They'd pumped him full of powerful drugs, shaved his head, performed surgery, and placed syringes into Akol's skull—all desperate attempts to drain the fluid and save his life—but had not managed to bring the fever down.

A week after he was admitted, we got a call from Wendy. The doctors had news and wanted his family and those close to him at the hospital immediately. As the principal, it was my duty to go as well, and so reluctantly I went for the first time to the intensive care unit at Children's Hospital—a rambling, low-rise concrete building in a residential area south of the city core. I parked, entered the building, and made my way through the maze of hallways, past the cots and bassinets, until I reached the ICU.

The pediatric intensive care unit at Children's Hospital is a miraculous, wonderful, terrible place, a place no parent should ever have to see. There were few individual rooms and little sense of privacy as the doctors and nurses hurried about their work amid the beeping, chirping machines and monitors. I looked around and tried to get my bearings as I walked past the dozen beds or so that filled the ward, each full with a little child.

I saw one little boy and I guessed him to be about eighteen months old, the same age as my own son at the time. His eyes were closed, his tiny chest rising and falling to the beat of the ventilator, fighting to keep what little life he had left. His mother and father sat beside him, gaunt, helpless, and heartbroken. I felt horrible, eavesdropping on the most private, tender, awful moment any parent would ever face, and I tried my best to block out the cries of anguish that surrounded me and focused on searching for Akol.

I found him in a private room just off the ICU. He lay still in his bed, wires and tubes draped like a spider's web around him. I walked up, squeezed his hand, and said hello but he didn't respond. "He's comfortable. That's about all we can do for him now," a voice said behind me. I turned around to see a woman with kind eyes who introduced herself as the hospital social worker. She told me that, although I was currently his only visitor, a steady stream had been to see Akol every day since he'd been admitted.

We sat in her office and made small talk, mostly about Akol and his life and what he'd been like before he fell ill. She told me that the hospital staff had really taken to him, and although she'd seen thousands of sick children over the years, she'd rarely seen so many different people come in for one child. Then someone knocked on her door and, very soon, the place was full. Mary arrived with some friends from the Sudanese community. Akol's foster parents came not long after, as did Elin and various people who'd supported the family since their arrival. They were here to listen to what the doctor had to say, and the news was heartbreaking.

The damage to his brain was catastrophic and ongoing, and despite the best efforts of the hospital staff—the finest, most compassionate doctors and nurses in the province—they had been unable to break his infection. There was now no brain activity. There would be no cure or happy ending. Mary looked at her little boy hooked up to the ventilator and wept. Akol was a fighter and had been all his life, but this, she realized, was a battle he could not win. She screamed in anguish and fell to the floor weeping as the rest of us quietly slipped out of the room, giving Mary the time she needed to be alone with her son.

A few minutes later, the doctor, Mary, and one of her friends retired to a private room to discuss options. When they returned an hour later, we learned the decision. No heroic measures would be taken, the ventilation tube would be removed, and Akol would be kept comfortable until he died.

While they removed the tube, Elin and I waited outside in the hallway with the others. We stood by a large window and, though on a clear day the view would have been beautiful, today a mist had swept in, obscuring the city and the mountains, and a cold, grey rain fell onto the flat gravel roof of the hospital and pelted the glass. I felt at that moment that the rain was God's tears—and God was crying for Akol too.

The door opened and we were ushered back in. Akol lay still on the bed, his breath gurgled and intermittent, all the monitors removed. There was, after all, nothing more they could tell the medical staff. Mary sat beside Akol, her little baby daughter sleeping peacefully beside her. She held her son's hand and stroked the scars on his wounded head. Another breath came, faint and ragged, and then his chest was still for what seemed like a very long while before another came again.

The nurse looked at me, tears in his eyes, and whispered, "These are his last breaths. This is the end of life." And then, with Akol's cheek touching hers, Mary sang. I didn't understand the words but, in my mind, I like to think that she sang of Sudan and Africa, of Akol's ancestors and of the herds of cows that grazed the arid landscape. Like a warm desert wind, Mary's soft, beautiful voice filled the stillness of the hospital ward as she sang the last song of Akol Chol. She sang of his brave, short little life. She sang of his courage and his love for his brother and his little sister, only three months old and sleeping on the floor beside him. And perhaps she sang the song of Akol's father as well, swallowed up years ago by the madness of war. And, through my tears, I smiled because I knew his father was waiting out there patiently for him, and that neither would be alone again.

A few weeks passed and we grieved for Akol, collectively and alone in the deepest parts of ourselves. Then one day, a little boy of about the same age as Akol arrived at the school office with his mom. As Stephanie, Elin, and I greeted them, we saw that both wore the same fearful look we'd seen a hundred times on the faces of the newly arrived refugee students who'd shown up at our door. The boy's name was

Joe, and he was from Liberia. He and his mother had been in Canada for all of a week, had just settled in the neighbourhood and, like a thousand families before, had come to the school as quickly as they could.

"Sir, is there room in your school for me?" Joe asked timidly, crouching behind his mother. "I want very much to learn."

"I'm sorry," his mother added quickly, "I don't have much money to pay the fees, but I want my son to attend."

I quickly told Joe and his mom there were no fees and that he could start tomorrow. "And school supplies?" she asked, reaching into her purse, shocked that her child's education would be free. "How much are they? I can pay a little now."

"You don't have to pay a cent, just wait here a second please," I said, excusing myself as I ran to the storage room off our gym. Corporate sponsors had donated a significant number of backpacks full of supplies to us at the start of the year, and we still had several left. I grabbed one, then opened two others, and pooled all the supplies from three backpacks into one, hoping Doreen George, the community coordinator, wouldn't see me ransacking her packs. Job done and without witnesses, I hurried back to the office and gave it to the boy.

"Consider this a welcome to school present," I exclaimed. The thing must have weighed as much as he did, and when Joe opened it, he stared at the pencil crayons, felts, and erasers as if they were diamonds pulled from the earth.

"All mine?" Joe said in disbelief.

"All yours," I replied, my smile as big as his.

"So I can come to your school? There's a place for me?"

he asked again suspiciously, as if things were too good to be true.

"Edmonds is your school now, Joe," I told him, "and there's always room here for one more."

AFTERWORD

In September of 2010, Elin Horton was diagnosed with pancreatic cancer. She had felt tired for several months, lost weight, and developed diabetes. Her doctor had ordered tests and the results confirmed the most horrible news. Elin was young, only fifty-six—with a daughter just out of high school, a son in his early twenties, and her mother all living with her.

Her friends and family rallied around her and prayed but, despite chemotherapy, she got progressively weaker. By the spring she could no longer look after herself and knew it was time to consider another option—palliative care in a hospice. Elin was stoic and dignified throughout her journey, getting angry only when she thought of the terrible unfairness of how the cancer would rob her children of a mother, and her of the chance of seeing them grow up.

But her own family aside, Elin's thoughts were also on the children of Edmonds in those final weeks. I drove out to see her the night that Elaha won the public speaking contest. It was late, and it was only because I was acting on her strict orders that I gently pushed the door open and stepped into her quiet room.

"How'd Elaha do?" she asked softly.

"Won the whole thing," I replied.

"I knew it. That kid has quite the future in front of her," Elin replied, satisfied. "And how's Lois?" she added a few minutes later. The tall, intelligent, and exasperating Sudanese girl had always been one of Elin's favourites.

"Doing very well," I said, meaning it.

"Good," Elin replied before drifting back to sleep. "She's got quite a future ahead of her, too."

Elin Horton died June 3, 2011. This book stands as a tribute to the love and dedication she gave to her Edmonds family. She will be greatly missed.

To the entire staff of Edmonds Community School and Byrne Creek Secondary: Thank you for your tremendous hard work and the passion you bring to the job. The children and families of the Edmonds neighbourhood are lucky to have you.

To Peter Richmond and Patsy Graham in Agassiz: I learned so much from you.

To Lynne Archer and Ron Hall, my administrative partners in my years at Byrne Creek, and to Stephanie Miller and Dino Klarich, my vice principals at Edmonds Community School: Thank you.

To Al Post, my predecessor at Edmonds: You made the case why support was needed and they listened. I have done nothing except build on your work. The school and the families of Edmonds owe you a tremendous debt.

Additional words of gratitude to: Sarah Evans, Shannon Tirling, Doreen George, Peter Agg, Lorraine Hodgson, Rod Munch, Angela Basran, Ginny Tahara, Michelle LePoole, Nora Mora, Samina Edwards, Nancy Robson, Karen Dawson, Karolyn Washtock, Marg Zarin, Rene Sierra, Nancy Wong, and Pauline Wong.

Also, my sincere appreciation for the hard work of the Edmonds Community Council, especially: Shayma Akhi, Cathy Moroney, Pam Ventakaya, Tara Nagy, and Julia Snow.

A special thanks to: district staff members Patti Collins, Bev Ogilvie, Sheila Casselton, Deborah Simak, Pauline Meugens, Sue Dorey, Peter Van den Hoogen, Hafal Ahmad, Branka Vlasic, Winnie Yip, Judy Footman, Sandra Pandolfo, Rene Sierra, and Natalie Cutayne.

To the wonderful district maintenance and IT teams: Jay, Ian, Gord, Brian, Tommy, Scott, Sarah, Ken, Darwin, Johnson (I still want an iPhone!), and all the others who keep the building and the network running. Thank you.

To the Burnaby Board of Education and the senior administration team at the Burnaby School District: Chair Larry Hayes and trustee Diana Mumford in particular, superintendent Claudio Morelli, and assistant superintendents Gina Nicoli-Moen and Kevin Kardaal. Thank you for letting this book come to life and thank you for the extra support you provide to the children of Edmonds and Byrne Creek. In particular, I want to recognize retiring associate superintendent Elliot Grieve for his passion, kindness, and dedication to all community schools in Burnaby. That there is place in our schools for the families in this book is testament to his compassion and his vision.

I also would like to acknowledge the principals and vice principals at all schools in the Burnaby School District. You are a remarkable team of caring and dedicated educators.

Thank you as well to the amazing team of individuals, organizations, corporations and service clubs that help us provide the material resources and opportunities that our children deserve but would not otherwise receive. At the risk of missing someone, I want to acknowledge the work and kindness of: Gary Begin, Janice Froese, and the Deer Lake Rotary; Burnaby Lions; Burnaby Elks; Karen Doolan and Wendy Hampe; Manny Malhotra and the Vancouver Canucks; the Burnaby Fire Department and Burnaby RCMP; Jean Rasmussen, Mischa Greenwood, and the Canuck Family Education Centre; Telus; MoreSports; Night Hoops; Balloholics; Costco; The Vancouver Foundation; CUPE; Breakfast For Learning; John Buis and Basketball BC; Peggy Woodruff; Vicky Ma; Dancin' Stars Studio; Maggie Marquardt and South Burnaby Neighbourhood House; Chris Friesen, Naomi Staddon, and ISS; The Universal Gospel Choir; Annette and Lauren Vowles; Keith and Celia Rice-Jones; the Honorable Raj Choulhan; the Honorable Peter Julian; Constable Rebecca Munn; Dave Duckworth and Camp Jubilee; Helen Stolte—and everyone else who has helped pay for pencils, camp, hot lunch, and the host of other things you have supported over the years.

I would also like to recognize the terrific work of: the doctors, nurses, volunteers and staff at BC Children's Hospital, Royal Columbia Hospital, and especially the staff at the Langley hospice and Langley Memorial Hospital.

Finally, my deepest gratitude goes out to Diane Young,

the editorial director at Lorimer who signed up this book, editor Ginny Freeman MacOwan, photographers Lisa Snow and Jennifer Houghton, and the *Vancouver Province* serial thriller contest team—Ros Gucci, John Fuller, Lena Sin, Cheryl Chan, Daniel Kalla, and Natalia Aponte. Thank you for rekindling my crazy dream to one day write a book.